Mastering Amazon Web Services (AWS)

Kameron Hussain

Published by Kameron Hussain, 2023.

While every precaution has been taken in the preparation of this book, the publisher assumes no responsibility for errors or omissions, or for damages resulting from the use of the information contained herein.

MASTERING AMAZON WEB SERVICES (AWS)

First edition. October 3, 2023.

Copyright © 2023 Kameron Hussain.

ISBN: 979-8223959175

Written by Kameron Hussain.

Contents

MASTERING AMAZON WEB SERVICES

Example Code

Section 16.5: AI and ML Best Practices

1. Data Quality and Preparation

2. Model Selection

3. Data Security and Compliance

4. Model Training

5. Testing and Validation

6. Scalability and Deployment

7. Continuous Monitoring and Optimization

8. Cost Optimization

9. Documentation and Collaboration

10. AI Ethics and Bias Mitigation

11. Disaster Recovery and Backup

12. Training and Education

13. Stay Informed

Chapter 17: AWS Migration and Hybrid Cloud

Section 17.1: Cloud Migration Strategies

1. Rehosting (Lift and Shift)

2. Replatforming (Lift, Tinker, and Shift)

3. Refactoring (Rearchitecting)

4. Rebuilding

5. Hybrid Cloud Deployments

6. Data Migration

7. Testing and Validation

8. Cost Management

9. Security and Compliance

10. Training and Skills Development

Section 17.2: AWS Database Migration Service (DMS)

Key Features of AWS DMS

Steps to Perform a Database Migration with AWS DMS

Benefits of Using AWS DMS

1. Use AWS Cost Explorer
2. Leverage Cost Allocation Tags
3. Rightsize Your Resources
4. Reserved Instances (RIs) and Savings Plans
5. Spot Instances and Spot Fleets
6. Use Auto Scaling Effectively
7. Data Transfer Costs
8. Storage Optimization
9. Elastic Load Balancing
10. Implement a Cost Optimization Culture
11. Consider Serverless and Managed Services
12. Continuous Monitoring and Optimization

Chapter 19: Case Studies and Real-World Scenarios

Section 19.1: Case Study: Building a High-Performance
Website
Introduction
Challenges
AWS Solutions
Results
Section 19.2: Real-World Data Analytics with AWS
Challenges
AWS Solutions
Results
Section 19.3: IoT Implementation Success Story
Challenges
AWS IoT Solutions
Results
Section 19.4: Machine Learning in Healthcare
The Promise of Machine Learning in Healthcare
AWS Machine Learning Services
Use Cases

Chapter 1: Introduction to AWS

Section 1.1: What is Cloud Computing?

Cloud computing is a transformative technology that has revolutionized the way organizations and individuals manage and deliver computing resources. It enables access to a wide range of IT services and resources over the internet, providing scalability, flexibility, and cost-efficiency. In this section, we will delve into the fundamental concepts of cloud computing, its benefits, and key characteristics.

Cloud Computing Fundamentals

At its core, cloud computing is the delivery of computing services, including servers, storage, databases, networking, software, analytics, and more, over the internet. Instead of owning and maintaining physical hardware and software, users can access these resources on a pay-as-you-go basis, typically through a subscription model. This allows organizations to reduce capital expenditure and focus on their core business activities.

Key Characteristics of Cloud Computing

1. **On-Demand Self-Service**: Cloud resources can be provisioned and managed without requiring human intervention. Users can scale resources up or down as needed, often with just a few clicks.
2. **Broad Network Access**: Cloud services are accessible over the internet from a variety of devices, including laptops, smartphones, and tablets. This accessibility enables remote work and collaboration.
3. **Resource Pooling**: Cloud providers use multi-tenant

models to serve multiple customers from shared infrastructure. Resources are dynamically allocated and reassigned based on demand, optimizing resource utilization.

4. **Rapid Elasticity**: Cloud resources can be quickly and automatically scaled to accommodate changes in workload. This elasticity ensures that applications can handle traffic spikes without performance degradation.

5. **Measured Service**: Cloud usage is metered, and users are billed based on their consumption. This pay-as-you-go model provides cost transparency and cost control.

Cloud Service Models

Cloud computing offers several service models, each catering to different needs:

• **Infrastructure as a Service (IaaS)**: Provides virtualized computing resources over the internet. Users can rent virtual machines, storage, and networking components. Example: Amazon EC2.

• **Platform as a Service (PaaS)**: Offers a platform that includes development tools, databases, and middleware, enabling developers to build, deploy, and manage applications without worrying about infrastructure. Example: AWS Elastic Beanstalk.

• **Software as a Service (SaaS)**: Delivers software applications over the internet on a subscription basis. Users can access applications through a web browser without installation. Example: Gmail.

Cloud Deployment Models

Cloud services can be deployed in different ways to meet specific requirements:

- **Public Cloud**: Services are offered to the general public and are owned and operated by cloud service providers like AWS, Microsoft Azure, and Google Cloud. These services are accessible over the internet.

- **Private Cloud**: Resources are dedicated to a single organization and may be hosted on-premises or by a third-party provider. Private clouds offer more control and customization options.

- **Hybrid Cloud**: Combines public and private cloud resources, allowing data and applications to be shared between them. Hybrid clouds provide flexibility and scalability while maintaining control over sensitive data.

Benefits of Cloud Computing

Cloud computing offers numerous advantages, including:

- **Scalability**: Easily scale resources up or down based on demand, avoiding overprovisioning or underutilization.

- **Cost Savings**: Reduce capital expenditure on hardware and maintenance. Pay only for what you use.

- **Flexibility**: Quickly adapt to changing business needs by deploying new resources and services.

- **Accessibility**: Access data and applications from anywhere with an internet connection.

- **Security**: Cloud providers invest in robust security measures, often surpassing what individual organizations can achieve.

- **Innovation**: Leverage cutting-edge technologies and services without the need for significant upfront investment.

In summary, cloud computing is a game-changer in the world of IT, offering flexibility, scalability, and cost-efficiency. Understanding its core concepts and benefits is crucial for organizations looking to harness the power of the cloud for their digital transformation journey.

Section 1.2: Evolution of AWS

The evolution of Amazon Web Services (AWS) is a remarkable journey that has played a pivotal role in shaping the cloud computing landscape. In this section, we will explore the key milestones and transformations that AWS has undergone since its inception.

The Birth of AWS

AWS was officially launched by Amazon.com in 2006, although its origins can be traced back to a few years earlier. Jeff Bezos, Amazon's founder and CEO, recognized the potential of Amazon's extensive IT infrastructure and expertise in managing a massive online retail operation. He envisioned offering these capabilities to external customers, paving the way for AWS.

AWS Services Begin

The initial AWS offering included fundamental services like Amazon S3 (Simple Storage Service) for storage and Amazon EC2

(Elastic Compute Cloud) for computing. These services laid the foundation for cloud computing as we know it today. Amazon S3 revolutionized data storage by providing scalable, durable, and cost-effective object storage accessible via a simple API. Amazon EC2 introduced the concept of on-demand virtual servers, making it easier for businesses to scale their computing resources.

Pioneering the Cloud

AWS quickly gained traction, attracting startups and enterprises alike. Its pay-as-you-go pricing model and the ability to provision resources on-demand resonated with businesses seeking agility and cost-efficiency. AWS continued to expand its service portfolio, introducing services for databases, content delivery, and more.

The Launch of Amazon VPC

In 2009, Amazon Virtual Private Cloud (Amazon VPC) was introduced, allowing customers to create isolated network environments within the AWS cloud. This feature addressed security and networking concerns, making AWS suitable for a wider range of applications, including those with strict compliance requirements.

Global Expansion

AWS didn't confine itself to a single region. It expanded globally, establishing data centers in multiple regions around the world. This global infrastructure allowed customers to deploy their applications closer to their end-users, improving latency and reliability.

AWS Marketplace and Partner Ecosystem

To further enhance its ecosystem, AWS introduced the AWS Marketplace, a platform for buying and selling software and services that complement AWS offerings. Additionally, AWS cultivated a vast partner network, including technology partners, consulting partners, and managed service providers, to assist customers in their cloud journey.

Innovation and Specialization

AWS has continued to innovate, launching specialized services for machine learning, analytics, IoT, and more. Amazon SageMaker, AWS Lambda, and Amazon Redshift are just a few examples of services that have pushed the boundaries of what is possible in the cloud.

Enterprise Adoption

Enterprises across various industries, including healthcare, finance, and media, have embraced AWS for mission-critical workloads. AWS provides compliance certifications and security features that meet the stringent requirements of these sectors.

Conclusion

The evolution of AWS has been characterized by continuous innovation, global expansion, and a commitment to customer success. From its humble beginnings as an online bookstore to becoming the world's leading cloud provider, AWS has redefined the IT landscape, enabling organizations of all sizes to harness the power of the cloud for their digital transformation journeys.

Section 1.3: AWS Global Infrastructure

Amazon Web Services (AWS) operates one of the most extensive and geographically diverse cloud infrastructures in the world. In this section, we will explore the AWS global infrastructure, which is a critical component of AWS's ability to deliver reliable and scalable cloud services.

Regions and Availability Zones

AWS's global infrastructure is organized into regions and availability zones. A region is a geographic area that consists of multiple, isolated data centers called availability zones. Each availability zone is equipped with its own power, cooling, and networking infrastructure. Regions are designed to be completely independent of one another, offering redundancy and failover capabilities.

Example:
- US East (N. Virginia) Region
- Availability Zone: us-east-1a
- Availability Zone: us-east-1b
- Availability Zone: us-east-1c

Edge Locations and CloudFront

In addition to regions and availability zones, AWS has a network of edge locations that are part of the Amazon CloudFront content delivery network (CDN). Edge locations are distributed globally and are strategically placed to reduce latency for content delivery, such as web pages and streaming media. They also play a role in the distribution of AWS services.

Example:
- Edge Location: New York City
- Edge Location: London
- Edge Location: Tokyo

Benefits of a Global Infrastructure

1. **High Availability**: AWS's use of multiple availability zones within regions ensures high availability and fault tolerance. Applications can be designed to run across multiple availability zones for redundancy.
2. **Low Latency**: Edge locations reduce latency for content

delivery, improving the user experience for applications and websites served through CloudFront.

3. **Data Residency and Compliance**: Customers can choose regions where their data will be stored, helping them meet data residency and compliance requirements.
4. **Disaster Recovery**: AWS's global infrastructure provides a foundation for robust disaster recovery strategies. Data can be replicated across regions for business continuity.
5. **Global Reach**: Organizations can deploy applications and services closer to their global user base, reducing the distance data must travel and improving performance.

Region and Availability Zone Selection

When using AWS services, selecting the right region and availability zone(s) is crucial. Factors to consider include:

- **Proximity to Users**: Choose a region that is geographically close to your users to minimize latency.

- **Data Residency**: Ensure that the region you select complies with data residency regulations relevant to your organization.

- **Redundancy**: Use multiple availability zones for high availability. AWS provides tools like Elastic Load Balancing (ELB) to distribute traffic across availability zones.

- **Service Availability**: Not all AWS services are available in every region. Check the AWS Regional Services List for service availability by region.

AWS Global Accelerator

AWS Global Accelerator is a service that helps improve the availability and performance of applications by using static IP addresses (Anycast) that route traffic over the AWS global network to optimal AWS endpoints based on health, geography, and routing policies. It simplifies global traffic management and provides failover capabilities.

In conclusion, AWS's global infrastructure, consisting of regions, availability zones, edge locations, and services like AWS Global Accelerator, forms the backbone of AWS's cloud offerings. Understanding how to leverage this infrastructure is essential for designing highly available, scalable, and performant cloud applications.

Section 1.4: AWS Service Categories

Amazon Web Services (AWS) offers a wide range of cloud services, each designed to address specific computing needs. These services can be categorized into several key service categories. In this section, we will explore these categories and provide an overview of the services they encompass.

1. Compute Services

Compute services in AWS provide scalable and flexible computing resources. They include:

- **Amazon EC2 (Elastic Compute Cloud)**: Virtual servers in the cloud that can be configured with various operating systems and instance types.

- **AWS Lambda**: A serverless compute service that runs code in response to events without the need to provision servers.

- **Amazon ECS (Elastic Container Service)**: A container orchestration service for managing Docker containers.

- **Amazon Elastic Beanstalk**: A platform as a service (PaaS) that simplifies the deployment and management of applications.

2. Storage Services

AWS storage services provide options for storing and managing data. Key services include:

- **Amazon S3 (Simple Storage Service)**: Object storage designed for scalability, durability, and data availability.

- **Amazon EBS (Elastic Block Store)**: Block storage volumes for use with Amazon EC2 instances.

- **Amazon Glacier**: A low-cost, long-term data archiving service.

- **Amazon EFS (Elastic File System)**: A scalable file storage service for use with Amazon EC2 instances.

3. Networking and Content Delivery

Networking and content delivery services facilitate network connectivity and data distribution. These services include:

- **Amazon VPC (Virtual Private Cloud)**: A virtual network that enables isolation and security for AWS resources.

- **Amazon Route 53**: A scalable domain name system (DNS) web service.

- **Elastic Load Balancing**: A service for distributing incoming traffic across multiple EC2 instances.

- **Amazon CloudFront**: A content delivery network (CDN) service for distributing content globally.

4. Database Services

AWS offers a variety of database services to meet different requirements:

- **Amazon RDS (Relational Database Service)**: Managed database service supporting multiple database engines, including MySQL, PostgreSQL, and SQL Server.

- **Amazon DynamoDB**: A fully managed NoSQL database service for applications that need seamless scalability.

- **Amazon Redshift**: A data warehousing service for running complex analytical queries on large datasets.

- **Amazon Aurora**: A high-performance, fully managed relational database engine compatible with MySQL and PostgreSQL.

5. Security and Identity Services

AWS provides robust security and identity services to protect resources and data:

- **Identity and Access Management (IAM)**: A service for managing user access to AWS resources through policies and permissions.

- **Security Groups and NACLs**: Network security features for controlling inbound and outbound traffic.

- **AWS Inspector and Trusted Advisor**: Services for security assessments and best practices recommendations.

- **Encryption and Key Management**: Tools for data encryption and secure key storage.

6. Monitoring and Management Tools

Monitoring and management services help users track and optimize their AWS resources:

- **Amazon CloudWatch**: A monitoring service for collecting and analyzing metrics and logs.

- **AWS CloudTrail**: A service for logging and auditing API calls made on AWS resources.

- **AWS Config**: A configuration management service for assessing, auditing, and evaluating resource configurations.

- **AWS Systems Manager**: A unified user interface for centralizing operational data and tasks.

7. Automation and Orchestration

Automation services enable the management and provisioning of resources through code:

- **AWS CloudFormation**: A service for defining and deploying infrastructure as code.

- **AWS Elastic Beanstalk**: A platform for deploying and managing applications in various programming languages.

- **AWS Step Functions**: A serverless orchestration service for coordinating AWS services.

- **Serverless Application Model (SAM)**: A framework for building serverless applications.

8. High Availability and Scalability

AWS provides services and features for achieving high availability and scalability:

- **AWS Auto Scaling**: A service for automatically adjusting the capacity of EC2 instances based on demand.

- **Amazon Elastic Load Balancing**: A load balancing service that distributes traffic across multiple instances.

- **Multi-AZ Deployments**: Deploy resources in multiple availability zones for redundancy.

- **Content Delivery and Caching**: Use services like Amazon CloudFront and Amazon ElastiCache for improved content delivery and caching.

9. Cost Optimization

Cost optimization services and best practices help organizations manage their AWS spending:

- **AWS Cost Explorer**: A tool for visualizing and analyzing AWS cost and usage data.

- **Cost Allocation Tags**: Labels for tracking and organizing AWS resource costs.

- **EC2 Instance Types and Pricing**: Choose the right instance types and pricing models to optimize costs.

- **Reserved Instances and Savings Plans**: Reserved capacity options for cost savings.

10. Other Service Categories

AWS also offers services in categories such as serverless computing, big data and analytics, Internet of Things (IoT), machine learning, migration and hybrid cloud, well-architected frameworks, and more. These services cater to diverse business needs and application scenarios.

In summary, AWS provides a comprehensive set of services across various categories, empowering organizations to build, deploy, and manage applications and infrastructure in the cloud. Understanding these service categories is essential for making informed decisions when architecting solutions on AWS.

Section 1.5: Getting Started with AWS

Getting started with Amazon Web Services (AWS) is an exciting journey that begins with the creation of an AWS account and gaining access to a wide array of cloud services. In this section, we will walk you through the initial steps to set up your AWS account and provide an overview of essential concepts for beginners.

Creating an AWS Account

To begin your AWS journey, you need to create an AWS account. Follow these steps:

1. Visit the AWS Sign-Up Page[1] and click "Create an AWS Account."
2. Provide the necessary information, including your email address, password, and account name.
3. Enter your contact information and payment details. AWS offers a Free Tier with limited resources for the first 12 months, allowing you to explore many services at no cost.
4. Once your account is created, you will receive an email with instructions for verification.
5. Sign in to the AWS Management Console using your new AWS account credentials.

AWS Identity and Access Management (IAM)

IAM is a fundamental service in AWS that allows you to manage user access to AWS resources securely. Here are some key concepts:

- **Users**: Create IAM users for individuals or services that need access to your AWS account.

- **Groups**: Organize users into groups with common permissions.

- **Roles**: Define roles with specific permissions for AWS services or resources.

---

1. https://aws.amazon.com/

- **Policies**: Attach policies to users, groups, or roles to grant permissions.

Billing and Cost Management

Understanding AWS billing is crucial to managing costs effectively. Some key points to keep in mind:

- Monitor your AWS spending using AWS Cost Explorer.

- Set up billing alerts to receive notifications when your costs exceed predefined thresholds.

- Use cost allocation tags to categorize resources for cost tracking.

- Review the AWS Free Tier to identify services that are available at no cost for new accounts.

Security Best Practices

Security is a top priority in AWS. Follow these best practices:

- Enable multi-factor authentication (MFA) for your AWS account.

- Apply the principle of least privilege when granting permissions through IAM.

- Regularly rotate access keys and passwords.

- Keep your AWS resources, including S3 buckets and EC2 instances, private by default.

Configuring Multi-Factor Authentication (MFA)

MFA adds an extra layer of security to your AWS account. Here's how to set it up:

1. Sign in to the AWS Management Console.
2. Open the IAM dashboard.
3. In the navigation pane, choose "Users."
4. Select the user to which you want to add MFA.
5. Choose the "Security credentials" tab, then click "Manage" in the "Assigned MFA device" section.
6. Follow the on-screen instructions to configure MFA for the user.

Accessing the AWS Management Console

Once your account is set up, you can access the AWS Management Console, a web-based interface for managing your AWS resources. Here's how to access it:

1. Go to the AWS Management Console[2].
2. Sign in using your AWS account credentials.
3. You'll be presented with a dashboard where you can navigate to various AWS services and resources.

AWS Command Line Interface (CLI)

The AWS CLI allows you to interact with AWS services from the command line. You can install it on your local machine and configure it to work with your AWS account. Here's how to get started:

1. Install the AWS CLI by following the instructions for your operating system. You can find installation guides in the

---

2. https://aws.amazon.com/console/

AWS CLI User Guide[3].

2. After installation, open a terminal or command prompt and run aws configure to set up your AWS credentials and default region.

AWS Software Development Kits (SDKs)

AWS provides SDKs for various programming languages, making it easier to integrate AWS services into your applications. You can find SDKs for languages like Python, Java, JavaScript, and more in the AWS SDKs and Tools[4] section of the AWS website.

In summary, getting started with AWS involves creating an AWS account, setting up IAM users and roles, understanding billing and cost management, implementing security best practices, and accessing AWS services through the AWS Management Console, CLI, or SDKs. These initial steps lay the foundation for your AWS journey, whether you're exploring cloud concepts, developing applications, or managing infrastructure in the cloud.

---

3. https://docs.aws.amazon.com/cli/latest/userguide/cli-configure-files.html

4. https://aws.amazon.com/tools/

Chapter 2: Setting Up Your AWS Account

Section 2.1: Creating an AWS Account

Creating an AWS account is the first step towards leveraging Amazon Web Services (AWS) for your cloud computing needs. In this section, we'll walk you through the process of creating an AWS account, ensuring you have access to the powerful suite of AWS services.

Why Create an AWS Account?

An AWS account is necessary to access and use AWS services. Here are some compelling reasons to create one:

1. **Access to the AWS Free Tier**: AWS offers a Free Tier with limited access to various services for the first 12 months. This is an excellent way to explore AWS at no cost.
2. **Scalable Computing Resources**: With an AWS account, you can provision virtual servers, known as Amazon Elastic Compute Cloud (EC2) instances, and scale your compute resources as needed.
3. **Data Storage and Databases**: AWS provides services like Amazon Simple Storage Service (S3) for object storage and Amazon Relational Database Service (RDS) for managed databases.
4. **AI and Machine Learning**: Utilize AWS services such as Amazon SageMaker for machine learning projects.
5. **Global Infrastructure**: Access a global network of data centers and content delivery to reach users worldwide.

Steps to Create an AWS Account

Follow these steps to create your AWS account:

1. **Visit the AWS Sign-Up Page**: Go to the AWS Sign-Up Page[5] to start the account creation process.
2. **Click "Create an AWS Account"**: Locate the "Create an AWS Account" button and click on it to begin.
3. **Provide Account Information**: Fill in your email address, password, and an AWS account name. The account name is a unique identifier for your AWS account.
4. **Contact Information**: Enter your contact information, including your name, company name, and phone number.
5. **Payment Information**: Provide your payment information. AWS may charge a small verification fee, which will be refunded to your account.
6. **Identity Verification**: AWS will verify your identity by sending a verification code to the phone number you provided. Enter the code to complete the verification.
7. **Choose a Support Plan**: You can choose from various support plans, including the Basic Support Plan, which is free. Select the one that suits your needs.
8. **Confirmation**: Review the information you provided and click "Create Account and Continue" to create your AWS account.
9. **Welcome to AWS**: Once your account is created, you'll receive a welcome email, and you can start using AWS services.

AWS Free Tier

As mentioned earlier, AWS offers a Free Tier that allows you to use many AWS services at no cost for the first 12 months. Some services

---

5. https://aws.amazon.com/

are always free, while others have usage limits that you should be aware of. The AWS Free Tier is an excellent way to explore and learn AWS without incurring charges.

Managing Your AWS Account

After creating your AWS account, you can access the AWS Management Console, a web-based interface for managing your AWS resources. Here, you can create, configure, and manage services, set up security, and monitor your usage and billing.

Conclusion

Creating an AWS account is a straightforward process that opens the door to a vast array of cloud services and resources. It's the first step on your journey to harnessing the power of AWS for your projects, whether they involve web hosting, data analysis, machine learning, or any other cloud computing endeavor.

Section 2.2: AWS Identity and Access Management (IAM)

Amazon Web Services Identity and Access Management (AWS IAM) is a crucial service for managing user access and permissions within your AWS account. IAM allows you to control who can access AWS resources and what actions they can perform. In this section, we'll dive into the key concepts and best practices of AWS IAM.

IAM Concepts

Users

IAM users represent individuals or entities that interact with AWS resources. Each user has their own set of security credentials (access keys or passwords) and permissions. IAM users are typically associated with human users, such as administrators, developers, or operators.

Groups

Groups are collections of IAM users. By associating users with groups, you can manage permissions for multiple users simultaneously. For example, you can create a "Developers" group and grant it permissions to access specific AWS resources.

Roles

IAM roles are used to delegate permissions to AWS services, EC2 instances, or other trusted entities. Roles are often used in scenarios where an EC2 instance needs access to other AWS services or when AWS Lambda functions require specific permissions.

Policies

IAM policies are JSON documents that define the permissions granted to users, groups, or roles. Policies specify the actions allowed or denied on AWS resources and the conditions under which these permissions apply.

IAM Best Practices

1. **Use the Principle of Least Privilege**: Grant users, groups, or roles the minimum permissions required to perform their tasks. Avoid over-privileged accounts, which can lead to security vulnerabilities.

2. **Regularly Review and Audit Permissions**: Periodically review and audit IAM policies and permissions to ensure they are up-to-date and aligned with your organization's needs. AWS provides tools like IAM Access Analyzer to help identify unintended access.

3. **Enable Multi-Factor Authentication (MFA)**: Require MFA for IAM users to add an extra layer of security. This ensures that even if an access key or password is compromised, an attacker still cannot access resources without the MFA code.

4. **Use IAM Roles for EC2 Instances**: When running applications on Amazon EC2 instances, use IAM roles to grant permissions to instances rather than embedding access keys within instances. IAM roles provide automatic key rotation and enhance security.

5. **Use IAM Roles for Cross-Account Access**: When accessing resources in another AWS account, use IAM roles with cross-account trust instead of sharing access keys. This improves security and allows for easier revocation of access.

6. **Implement Strong Password Policies**: Enforce strong password policies for IAM users, including password complexity and rotation requirements.

7. **Implement IAM Policies with Conditions**: Fine-tune permissions using IAM policies with conditions. For example, you can restrict access based on IP addresses or

time of day.

8. **Monitor and Log IAM Activity**: Enable AWS CloudTrail to capture IAM actions for auditing and security analysis. Use Amazon CloudWatch Logs to monitor and analyze IAM activity in real-time.

IAM Access Keys

IAM users can access AWS programmatically using access keys (access key ID and secret access key). When creating access keys for users, ensure they are stored securely. Avoid hardcoding access keys in code or configuration files, as this can pose a security risk.

```
# AWS CLI command to create an IAM access key for a user
aws iam create-access-key—user-name <user-name>
```

IAM Roles

IAM roles are essential for granting permissions to AWS services and EC2 instances. When creating an IAM role, specify trusted entities and define permissions in the role's policy.

```
{
"Version": "2012-10-17",
"Statement": [
{
"Effect": "Allow",
"Action": "s3:GetObject",
"Resource": "arn:aws:s3:::my-bucket/*"
}
]
}
```

IAM roles can be assumed by AWS services or users, depending on the use case. For example, an EC2 instance can assume an IAM role to access an S3 bucket securely.

IAM Policies

IAM policies are JSON documents that define permissions. They consist of statements with an "Effect" (Allow/Deny), "Action" (e.g., s3:GetObject), and "Resource" (e.g., ARN of an S3 bucket or object). Policies can be attached to users, groups, or roles.

```
{
"Version": "2012-10-17",
"Statement": [
{
"Effect": "Allow",
"Action": "s3:GetObject",
"Resource": "arn:aws:s3:::my-bucket/*"
}
]
}
```

Conclusion

AWS Identity and Access Management (IAM) is a fundamental service for managing user access and permissions within AWS. Implementing IAM best practices, using IAM roles, and monitoring IAM activity are essential steps to enhance the security and manageability of your AWS resources. By following these guidelines, you can ensure that users and applications have the right level of access while maintaining a robust security posture.

Section 2.3: Billing and Cost Management

Managing your AWS billing and costs is a critical aspect of using Amazon Web Services effectively. In this section, we will explore various aspects of billing and cost management in AWS, including cost visibility, budgeting, and cost optimization strategies.

AWS Billing Basics

AWS operates on a pay-as-you-go pricing model, where you are billed only for the resources and services you use. To understand your AWS billing:

1. **Billing Dashboard**: The AWS Management Console provides a Billing Dashboard that offers an overview of your current and past bills. You can access it by navigating to "Billing & Cost Management."
2. **Cost Explorer**: AWS Cost Explorer is a tool that allows you to visualize and analyze your AWS spending over time. It provides insights into your costs, usage, and helps identify cost trends.
3. **Detailed Billing Reports**: AWS generates detailed billing reports in CSV format, providing granular information about your resource usage and associated costs. These reports can be downloaded from the AWS Billing Dashboard.

AWS Free Tier

AWS offers a Free Tier for new accounts, allowing you to use a range of AWS services for free during your first 12 months. Some services are always free, while others have usage limits within the Free Tier. It's essential to review the AWS Free Tier offerings to understand which services are available at no cost.

AWS Budgets

AWS Budgets is a feature that helps you set spending limits and track your AWS costs. You can create budgets based on different criteria, such as service, linked account, or cost and usage type. AWS can send alerts when your costs exceed predefined thresholds, helping you stay within your budget.

AWS Cost Allocation Tags

Cost allocation tags are labels that you can apply to your AWS resources to categorize and track your spending. You can use tags to allocate costs to specific departments, projects, or teams within your organization. This makes it easier to understand how different areas are contributing to your overall AWS expenses.

AWS Organizations

AWS Organizations is a service that allows you to manage multiple AWS accounts within your organization. It simplifies the process of managing billing and cost allocation across accounts. You can set up consolidated billing, which combines the charges of all linked accounts into a single payment.

AWS Cost Optimization Strategies

Cost optimization in AWS involves finding ways to reduce your AWS spending while maintaining or improving your application's performance. Here are some cost optimization strategies:

1. **Rightsize Resources**: Choose the right instance types and sizes based on your application's actual needs. AWS offers various instance families optimized for different workloads.
2. **Reserved Instances (RIs) and Savings Plans**: RIs and Savings Plans offer significant cost savings compared to on-demand pricing. Consider purchasing them for predictable workloads.
3. **Auto Scaling**: Implement auto scaling to automatically

adjust the number of instances based on demand, ensuring you only pay for what you need.

4. **Use Spot Instances**: For workloads with flexible timing and capacity requirements, consider using EC2 Spot Instances, which are significantly cheaper but can be interrupted.

5. **Data Transfer Costs**: Be mindful of data transfer costs, especially if your application involves transferring large amounts of data between regions or outside AWS.

6. **Use AWS Trusted Advisor**: AWS Trusted Advisor provides recommendations for cost optimization based on your usage patterns. It covers areas such as underutilized instances and idle resources.

7. **Monitor Resource Utilization**: Regularly monitor your resource utilization and identify underutilized or over-provisioned resources. Make adjustments accordingly.

AWS Cost Explorer

AWS Cost Explorer is a powerful tool for visualizing and analyzing your AWS spending. You can use it to create custom cost and usage reports, set up budgets, and view cost and usage data by services, linked accounts, and more.

Conclusion

Effective billing and cost management are essential for maximizing the value of AWS while controlling expenses. By using AWS budgeting, cost allocation tags, and implementing cost optimization strategies, you can gain better visibility into your costs, allocate expenses accurately, and optimize your AWS spending. Monitoring and adjusting your resource usage based on actual needs will help you achieve a cost-efficient AWS infrastructure.

Section 2.4: Security Best Practices

Security is a paramount concern when using Amazon Web Services (AWS). AWS provides a robust set of security features and services, but it's essential to understand and implement security best practices to protect your data and resources. In this section, we will discuss key security best practices for AWS.

1. Enable Multi-Factor Authentication (MFA)

Multi-Factor Authentication (MFA) adds an extra layer of security to your AWS account. When MFA is enabled, users must provide two or more authentication factors to access their accounts. This typically involves something you know (password) and something you have (a mobile device or hardware token).

To enable MFA for your AWS account:

1. Sign in to the AWS Management Console.
2. Open the IAM dashboard.
3. In the navigation pane, choose "Users."
4. Select the user for whom you want to enable MFA.
5. Choose the "Security credentials" tab.
6. In the "Multi-Factor Authentication (MFA)" section, click "Manage."
7. Follow the on-screen instructions to set up MFA for the user.

2. Use Identity and Access Management (IAM) Effectively

IAM allows you to control who can access your AWS resources and what actions they can perform. Here are some IAM best practices:

• Implement the principle of least privilege, granting users and roles only the permissions they need.

• Regularly review and audit IAM permissions to ensure they align with current requirements.

• Avoid sharing access keys or long-term credentials among users; use IAM roles instead.

• Use IAM roles for cross-account access to minimize security risks.

3. Secure Access Keys

Access keys (access key ID and secret access key) are used for programmatic access to AWS resources. To secure access keys:

• Rotate access keys regularly, especially if they are associated with IAM users or roles.

• Do not hardcode access keys in code or configuration files.

• Use AWS Identity and Access Management (IAM) roles for EC2 instances to avoid embedding access keys in instances.

4. Secure S3 Buckets

Amazon S3 (Simple Storage Service) is a popular AWS service for storing objects and files. To secure your S3 buckets:

• Configure bucket policies and access control lists (ACLs) to control who can access your data.

- Enable S3 bucket versioning to protect against accidental deletion of objects.

- Regularly review S3 bucket permissions to ensure they are set correctly.

5. Enable AWS CloudTrail

AWS CloudTrail logs API calls made on your AWS resources, providing valuable audit and security information. Enabling CloudTrail allows you to:

- Monitor and investigate suspicious activities and security incidents.
- Retain logs for compliance and auditing purposes.
- Use CloudWatch Alarms to get notified of specific events or patterns.

6. Implement Network Security

Use Amazon Virtual Private Cloud (VPC) to control network traffic and isolate resources. Best practices for network security include:

- Segregate resources into private and public subnets.

- Use security groups and network access control lists (NACLs) to control inbound and outbound traffic.

- Implement AWS Web Application Firewall (WAF) for web application protection.

- Use AWS Direct Connect or VPN for secure connections to on-premises data centers.

7. Encrypt Data

Encrypting sensitive data at rest and in transit is crucial. AWS offers various encryption options:

- Use server-side encryption (SSE) for data stored in S3, RDS, EBS, and other services.

- Enable SSL/TLS encryption for data transmitted over the network.

- Implement AWS Key Management Service (KMS) for managing encryption keys securely.

8. Monitor and Respond to Security Events

Implement continuous monitoring and incident response practices:

- Use Amazon CloudWatch and AWS Config for real-time monitoring.

- Set up alarms and notifications to detect and respond to security incidents.

- Establish an incident response plan and conduct security training and drills.

9. Regularly Update and Patch Resources

Keep your AWS resources, including EC2 instances and databases, up to date with the latest security patches and updates. Implement automated patch management solutions where possible.

10. Educate and Train Your Team

Security is a shared responsibility between AWS and your organization. Ensure that your team members are educated about AWS security best practices and regularly update their knowledge.

In conclusion, security should be a top priority when using AWS. By following these security best practices, you can mitigate risks, protect your data, and ensure the confidentiality, integrity, and availability of your AWS resources.

Section 2.5: Configuring Multi-Factor Authentication (MFA)

Multi-Factor Authentication (MFA) adds an extra layer of security to your AWS account by requiring users to provide two or more authentication factors to gain access. It significantly enhances the security of your AWS resources, especially for privileged accounts. In this section, we will discuss the importance of MFA and how to configure it for your AWS account.

The Importance of MFA

MFA is essential because it provides an additional barrier against unauthorized access to your AWS account, even if someone obtains your password or access key. Here's why MFA is crucial:

1. **Protects Against Unauthorized Access**: MFA requires something the user knows (password) and something the user has (a device or token). This makes it significantly more challenging for attackers to gain access.
2. **Mitigates the Risk of Stolen Credentials**: Even if your password is compromised, an attacker would also need access to your MFA device to log in successfully.
3. **Enhances Privileged Account Security**: For users with

elevated privileges, such as administrators, MFA is especially important to prevent unauthorized actions.

Configuring MFA for Your AWS Account

To configure MFA for your AWS account, follow these steps:

1. **Sign in to the AWS Management Console**: Use your AWS account's root user credentials to sign in to the AWS Management Console.
2. **Open the AWS Identity and Access Management (IAM) Dashboard**: From the AWS Management Console, navigate to the IAM dashboard.
3. **Access the Security Credentials Tab**: In the IAM dashboard, select the "Users" option in the navigation pane on the left. Then, select the user for whom you want to enable MFA.
4. **Manage MFA Device**: In the user details page, choose the "Security credentials" tab. Under the "Assigned MFA device" section, click "Manage."
5. **Configure MFA Device**: AWS provides options for configuring an MFA device:

– **Virtual MFA Device**: You can use a virtual MFA device, such as the Google Authenticator app or a compatible app. Select this option to scan a QR code with the MFA app.

– **Hardware MFA Device**: Alternatively, you can use a hardware MFA device, such as a physical MFA token.

1. **Complete the Setup**: Follow the on-screen instructions to complete the MFA device setup. This typically involves scanning a QR code or entering a provided key into your

MFA app.
2. **Verification**: After configuring your MFA device, AWS will prompt you to enter the current MFA code to verify that the device is working correctly.
3. **Save Configuration**: If verification is successful, save the MFA configuration.

Using MFA for AWS Account Access

Once MFA is enabled for your AWS account, you'll be required to provide the MFA code whenever you sign in to the AWS Management Console using your root user credentials. This code is generated by your MFA device and changes periodically.

Here's how using MFA works:

1. Sign in with your AWS root user credentials as usual.
2. When prompted, provide the MFA code generated by your MFA device.
3. Access to your AWS account is granted only if the MFA code is valid.

Managing and Replacing MFA Devices

It's important to manage your MFA devices and ensure you have a backup plan in case your primary MFA device is lost, stolen, or malfunctions. AWS allows you to:

- **Deactivate MFA**: If you no longer have access to your MFA device, you can deactivate it from the AWS Management Console.

- **Set Up a New MFA Device**: You can configure a new MFA device if needed.

- **Have Multiple MFA Devices**: AWS supports multiple MFA devices per user, providing redundancy.

Conclusion

Configuring Multi-Factor Authentication (MFA) for your AWS account is a crucial step in enhancing the security of your AWS resources. By requiring users to provide an additional authentication factor, MFA significantly reduces the risk of unauthorized access, protects against stolen credentials, and is particularly important for privileged accounts. It's a fundamental security practice that should be implemented and managed effectively to safeguard your AWS environment.

Chapter 3: AWS Compute Services

Section 3.1: Amazon EC2 (Elastic Compute Cloud)

Amazon Elastic Compute Cloud (Amazon EC2) is one of the foundational services of Amazon Web Services (AWS), providing scalable and resizable compute capacity in the cloud. In this section, we will explore Amazon EC2, its key features, and how to get started with deploying virtual servers in the AWS cloud.

What is Amazon EC2?

Amazon EC2 is a web service that allows you to run virtual servers, known as instances, in the AWS cloud. These instances can be used to host applications, run software, and perform various computing tasks. EC2 offers a wide range of instance types optimized for different workloads, ensuring you can choose the right combination of CPU, memory, storage, and networking resources for your applications.

Key Features of Amazon EC2:

1. Scalability

EC2 instances can be easily scaled up or down based on your application's demand. You can add or remove instances manually or use Auto Scaling to automate the process.

2. Variety of Instance Types

Amazon EC2 provides a broad selection of instance types optimized for various use cases, such as compute-optimized, memory-optimized, storage-optimized, and GPU instances.

3. Operating System Flexibility

You can choose from a variety of operating systems, including Amazon Linux, Windows Server, Ubuntu, and more. Additionally, you can import your custom images.

4. Security

EC2 instances can be placed within Virtual Private Clouds (VPCs) and secured using security groups and network ACLs. Key pairs are used for secure SSH (Linux) or RDP (Windows) access.

5. Data Storage Options

EC2 instances can be connected to various storage options, including Amazon Elastic Block Store (EBS) for block storage, Amazon S3 for object storage, and Amazon EFS for file storage.

6. Elastic Load Balancing

Amazon Elastic Load Balancing (ELB) can distribute incoming traffic across multiple EC2 instances to ensure high availability and fault tolerance.

7. Monitoring and Management

You can use Amazon CloudWatch to monitor the performance of your EC2 instances and set up alarms to respond to specific events.

Launching an EC2 Instance

Here are the basic steps to launch an EC2 instance:

1. **Sign in to the AWS Management Console**: Log in to your AWS account.
2. **Open the EC2 Dashboard**: Navigate to the EC2 dashboard in the AWS Management Console.
3. **Launch an Instance**: Click on the "Launch Instance" button to start the instance creation process.
4. **Choose an Amazon Machine Image (AMI)**: Select an AMI that corresponds to the operating system and software stack you need.
5. **Choose an Instance Type**: Choose an instance type based on your workload requirements.
6. **Configure Instance Details**: Set various instance options, including the number of instances, VPC settings, subnet, and more.
7. **Add Storage**: Define the storage volumes and configurations for your instance.
8. **Add Tags** (Optional): Add tags to your instance for better organization and identification.
9. **Configure Security Groups**: Define the security groups that control inbound and outbound traffic to your instance.
10. **Review and Launch**: Review your instance configuration, and click "Launch" to create your EC2 instance.
11. **Choose a Key Pair**: Select or create an SSH key pair (for

Linux) or a password (for Windows) to securely access your instance.

12. **Launch Instances**: Click "Launch Instances" to start your EC2 instance.

Once your EC2 instance is launched, you can connect to it using SSH or RDP, depending on the operating system, and begin using it for your specific applications and workloads.

Conclusion

Amazon EC2 is a fundamental AWS service that provides scalable and flexible compute capacity in the cloud. It allows you to create virtual servers tailored to your application's needs and offers a wide range of instance types and configurations. Understanding how to launch and manage EC2 instances is essential for anyone working with AWS cloud computing resources.

Section 3.2: AWS Lambda

AWS Lambda is a serverless computing service that lets you run code in response to events without the need to manage servers. It allows developers to build and deploy applications without worrying about server provisioning, scaling, or maintenance. In this section, we will explore AWS Lambda, its key features, and use cases.

Key Features of AWS Lambda:

1. Event-Driven Execution

Lambda functions are triggered by various AWS services or custom events. Common triggers include changes to objects in Amazon S3 buckets, updates to DynamoDB tables, incoming API Gateway requests, and more. This event-driven architecture allows you to build reactive applications.

2. No Server Management

With Lambda, you don't need to provision or manage servers. AWS takes care of server maintenance, scaling, patching, and monitoring. You only pay for the compute time consumed by your code.

3. Supported Runtimes

Lambda supports multiple programming languages, including Node.js, Python, Java, Ruby, Go, .NET Core, and custom runtimes. You can choose the runtime that best fits your application.

4. Easy Deployment

You can deploy Lambda functions using the AWS Management Console, AWS CLI, or AWS CloudFormation. Lambda automatically handles deployment versions, allowing you to manage and roll back to previous versions easily.

5. Integrated Security

Lambda functions run within an execution environment that is isolated from other functions. AWS Identity and Access Management (IAM) roles can be attached to Lambda functions to control their permissions and access to AWS resources.

6. Automatic Scaling

Lambda automatically scales your functions to handle incoming requests. You don't need to worry about configuring auto-scaling policies or managing the underlying infrastructure.

7. Monitoring and Logging

AWS provides built-in monitoring and logging capabilities for Lambda functions. You can use Amazon CloudWatch to view metrics, set up alarms, and monitor function performance. Lambda also supports custom logging to services like CloudWatch Logs.

8. Stateless Functions

Lambda functions are designed to be stateless. Any state that needs to be preserved should be stored in external services, such as Amazon DynamoDB or Amazon S3.

9. Cost-Effective

Lambda follows a pay-as-you-go pricing model, where you are billed based on the number of requests and the compute time your functions consume. This can lead to cost savings for workloads with varying or unpredictable traffic.

Use Cases for AWS Lambda:

1. Real-time Data Processing

Lambda can process data in real-time as it becomes available, making it suitable for tasks like stream processing, data validation, and transformation.

2. Automation

Automate repetitive tasks and workflows by triggering Lambda functions in response to events like scheduled events, changes in AWS resources, or incoming data.

3. Serverless APIs

Build serverless APIs using Amazon API Gateway and Lambda functions. This approach is cost-effective and highly scalable for handling web requests.

4. File and Data Processing

Lambda can be used to process files uploaded to Amazon S3, perform image and video transcoding, and execute ETL (Extract, Transform, Load) processes.

5. IoT Backend

Leverage Lambda to process data from Internet of Things (IoT) devices, perform real-time analytics, and send alerts or notifications.

6. Chatbots

Build serverless chatbots and conversational interfaces using services like Amazon Lex and Lambda to process user input and generate responses.

Creating a Lambda Function

Here's a high-level overview of how to create a Lambda function:

1. **Sign in to AWS**: Log in to the AWS Management Console.
2. **Open the Lambda Dashboard**: Navigate to the Lambda service in the AWS Management Console.
3. **Create a Function**: Click the "Create function" button.
4. **Configure the Function**: Provide a name for your function, choose a runtime, and specify the execution role (IAM role) that grants permissions to access other AWS resources.
5. **Add Triggers**: Configure event sources that will trigger your Lambda function. These can include S3 buckets, API Gateway, DynamoDB tables, and more.
6. **Write Code**: Write the code for your Lambda function directly in the Lambda Management Console using the integrated code editor or upload a deployment package.
7. **Test the Function**: You can test your function using the built-in test feature.
8. **Deploy the Function**: Once you're satisfied with your function, click "Deploy" to make it available for execution.
9. **Monitor and Manage**: Monitor your Lambda function's performance using CloudWatch and manage it as needed.

Conclusion

AWS Lambda is a powerful and versatile serverless computing service that allows you to build scalable and event-driven applications without the complexity of server management. By leveraging Lambda functions, developers can focus on writing code and responding to events, resulting in faster development cycles and cost-effective solutions for various use cases.

Section 3.3: Amazon ECS (Elastic Container Service)

Amazon Elastic Container Service (ECS) is a fully managed container orchestration service that allows you to run, scale, and manage Docker containers in the AWS cloud. ECS simplifies the deployment of containerized applications and provides a highly scalable and resilient platform. In this section, we will explore Amazon ECS, its core concepts, and how it can be used to manage containers.

Key Concepts of Amazon ECS:

1. Containers

Containers are lightweight, portable units that package applications and their dependencies. ECS enables you to run containers without worrying about the underlying infrastructure.

2. Tasks

A task in ECS represents a set of containers that run together on the same host. Tasks can be thought of as the basic unit of work in ECS.

You define tasks using task definitions, which specify the containers, their images, and their configurations.

3. Task Definitions

A task definition is a blueprint for your application, describing which Docker containers should run, what resources they need, and how they interact with each other. Task definitions are versioned and can be used to launch multiple tasks.

4. Services

ECS services allow you to define long-running applications that are automatically scheduled and maintained. Services ensure that a specified number of tasks are running and automatically replace any failed tasks.

5. Clusters

ECS clusters are logical groupings of EC2 instances or AWS Fargate resources that run your tasks. Clusters provide the underlying compute capacity for your containers.

6. Launch Types

ECS supports two launch types: EC2 and AWS Fargate. - **EC2**: In EC2 launch type, you run containers on your own EC2 instances that you manage. - **Fargate**: With Fargate, AWS manages the infrastructure, and you only need to specify your container requirements.

How to Use Amazon ECS:

1. Define a Task

Start by creating a task definition that specifies the containers, their images, and any resource requirements. You can define multiple task definitions for different parts of your application.

2. Create a Cluster

Set up an ECS cluster, either by using your existing EC2 instances or by selecting AWS Fargate as the launch type. The cluster provides the compute resources for your tasks.

3. Launch Tasks

Launch tasks in your cluster by specifying the task definition to use. ECS will automatically start the containers as tasks on available instances or Fargate resources.

4. Create a Service

For long-running applications, create an ECS service. A service ensures that a specified number of tasks are running and automatically replaces any failed tasks to maintain the desired state.

5. Scale and Load Balance

ECS provides auto-scaling options for services to automatically adjust the number of tasks based on demand. You can also use Amazon Elastic Load Balancing (ELB) to distribute incoming traffic across containers.

6. Monitor and Manage

Monitor the performance of your containers and clusters using Amazon CloudWatch. ECS integrates with CloudWatch to provide container-level and task-level metrics.

7. Update and Rollback

ECS supports updates to task definitions, allowing you to roll out changes to your application without downtime. You can also roll back to previous versions if issues arise.

Use Cases for Amazon ECS:

1. Microservices Architecture

ECS is well-suited for microservices-based applications, where different parts of the application run in separate containers. It allows you to scale and manage individual services independently.

2. Batch Processing

ECS can be used for batch processing workloads, such as data processing, image rendering, and video transcoding. Tasks can be scheduled to run on available resources as needed.

3. Web Applications

ECS is commonly used to deploy web applications and APIs. Services can automatically balance traffic and maintain the desired number of containers, ensuring high availability.

4. Continuous Integration and Continuous Deployment (CI/CD)

Integrate ECS into your CI/CD pipelines to automate the deployment of containerized applications. This enables rapid and reliable application updates.

Conclusion

Amazon ECS simplifies the management of Docker containers in the AWS cloud, allowing you to focus on developing and deploying applications without the burden of infrastructure management. By understanding the core concepts of ECS and its use cases, you can efficiently deploy and manage containerized applications at scale.

Section 3.4: Amazon Elastic Beanstalk

Amazon Elastic Beanstalk is a Platform-as-a-Service (PaaS) offering from AWS that simplifies the deployment, scaling, and management of web applications. With Elastic Beanstalk, developers can focus on writing code while AWS handles the underlying infrastructure. In this section, we will explore Amazon Elastic Beanstalk, its key features, and how to use it for deploying and managing web applications.

Key Features of Amazon Elastic Beanstalk:

1. Supported Programming Languages

Elastic Beanstalk supports a variety of programming languages and platforms, including Python, Java, Ruby, PHP, Node.js, .NET, and Go. You can choose the language that best suits your application.

2. Easy Application Deployment

Deploying applications on Elastic Beanstalk is straightforward. You provide your code, and Elastic Beanstalk takes care of provisioning resources, deploying the application, and setting up the required infrastructure components.

3. Environment Management

Elastic Beanstalk allows you to create multiple environments for your application, such as development, testing, and production. Each environment can have its own configuration settings, scaling options, and version deployments.

4. Auto Scaling

Elastic Beanstalk provides automatic scaling based on traffic and resource utilization. It can scale your application up or down to handle varying loads without manual intervention.

5. Integrated Monitoring and Logging

You can monitor the health and performance of your Elastic Beanstalk environments using Amazon CloudWatch. Elastic Beanstalk also provides integration with CloudWatch Logs for log management.

6. Load Balancing

Elastic Beanstalk can distribute incoming traffic across multiple instances using Elastic Load Balancing. This enhances availability and fault tolerance for your applications.

7. Database Integration

You can easily integrate your Elastic Beanstalk applications with AWS managed database services like Amazon RDS, Amazon DynamoDB, and Amazon ElastiCache.

8. Platform Customization

For advanced users, Elastic Beanstalk allows you to customize the underlying platform by providing configuration files. This enables you to install additional software or configure runtime settings.

Deploying a Web Application with Elastic Beanstalk:

Here are the basic steps to deploy a web application using Amazon Elastic Beanstalk:

1. **Sign in to AWS**: Log in to the AWS Management Console.
2. **Open the Elastic Beanstalk Dashboard**: Navigate to the Elastic Beanstalk service in the AWS Management Console.
3. **Create an Application**: Create a new Elastic Beanstalk application that represents your web application.
4. **Create an Environment**: Within your application, create an environment. You can choose from various environment types, such as web server environments, worker environments, or multi-container Docker environments.
5. **Configure Environment Settings**: Specify configuration settings for your environment, including the programming language, platform version, instance type, and scaling options.
6. **Upload Your Application Code**: Upload your web

application code or provide a source code repository link (e.g., from GitHub or AWS CodeCommit).

7. **Review and Launch**: Review the configuration settings, and click "Launch" to create your Elastic Beanstalk environment.
8. **Monitor and Manage**: Once your environment is running, you can monitor its performance, access logs, and make configuration changes as needed.

Use Cases for Amazon Elastic Beanstalk:

1. Web Applications

Elastic Beanstalk is commonly used for deploying and managing web applications, whether they are simple websites, web APIs, or complex web applications.

2. Microservices

Developers can use Elastic Beanstalk to deploy and manage individual microservices within a larger microservices architecture.

3. Staging and Testing Environments

Create separate Elastic Beanstalk environments for staging and testing to ensure changes are thoroughly tested before deploying to production.

4. Rapid Prototyping

Elastic Beanstalk is an excellent choice for quickly prototyping and launching web applications without the need for extensive infrastructure setup.

5. Scalable Web Services

For applications with varying traffic loads, Elastic Beanstalk's auto-scaling feature ensures that resources are automatically adjusted to handle demand.

Conclusion

Amazon Elastic Beanstalk provides a convenient and efficient way to deploy, manage, and scale web applications in the AWS cloud. By abstracting infrastructure management, Elastic Beanstalk allows developers to focus on writing code and delivering applications faster. Whether you are building a simple website, a complex web application, or a microservices-based architecture, Elastic Beanstalk can simplify the deployment process and improve application scalability and reliability.

Section 3.5: Choosing the Right Compute Service

When it comes to deploying applications in the cloud, AWS offers a variety of compute services, each designed for specific use cases and workloads. In this section, we will explore the considerations for choosing the right compute service among Amazon EC2, AWS Lambda, Amazon ECS, and Amazon Elastic Beanstalk.

Factors to Consider:

1. Workload Type

Consider the nature of your workload. Is it a traditional web application, a batch processing job, a serverless function, or a containerized microservices architecture? Each compute service is optimized for different workload types.

- **Amazon EC2**: Ideal for traditional applications where you need full control over the virtual machines, the operating system, and the software stack. EC2 instances are versatile and can run a wide range of applications.

- **AWS Lambda**: Suited for event-driven, serverless functions that execute in response to events or requests. Lambda is excellent for microservices, real-time data processing, and building serverless APIs.

- **Amazon ECS**: Designed for containerized workloads orchestrated with Docker. ECS is well-suited for applications that benefit from containerization, scalability, and ease of deployment.

- **Amazon Elastic Beanstalk**: A PaaS offering suitable for web applications, APIs, and microservices. Elastic Beanstalk abstracts infrastructure management and is ideal for rapid application deployment.

2. Scaling Requirements

Consider the scalability needs of your application. Do you anticipate fluctuating or unpredictable workloads? Each compute service offers different scaling capabilities.

- **Amazon EC2**: Allows you to manually or automatically scale instances based on traffic. EC2 is suitable for applications with varying workloads that may require vertical or horizontal scaling.

- **AWS Lambda**: Offers automatic scaling based on incoming events. Lambda functions automatically scale to handle the workload, making it well-suited for event-driven and unpredictable workloads.

- **Amazon ECS**: Supports auto-scaling for containers. You can define scaling policies based on CPU or memory utilization to automatically adjust the number of containers.

- **Amazon Elastic Beanstalk**: Provides auto-scaling options for web server environments. You can configure triggers based on CPU or request metrics to scale your application.

3. Management Complexity

Consider the level of control and management you want over your application's infrastructure. Different compute services offer varying degrees of control.

- **Amazon EC2**: Offers full control over the virtual machines, allowing you to configure the OS, install software, and manage updates. It's suitable for applications that require fine-grained control.

- **AWS Lambda**: Abstracts infrastructure management, allowing you to focus solely on code. Lambda is the least complex in terms of infrastructure management.

- **Amazon ECS**: Provides control over containerized applications and orchestration but abstracts the underlying infrastructure. It's a balance between control and ease of use.

- **Amazon Elastic Beanstalk**: Abstracts most of the infrastructure management, making it suitable for developers who want to deploy applications quickly with minimal configuration.

4. Cost Considerations

Evaluate the cost implications of your choice. Each compute service has its pricing model, and costs can vary based on factors like instance types, request rates, and resource usage.

- **Amazon EC2**: You pay for the provisioned compute capacity, which can be cost-effective for steady workloads but may not be the most economical choice for highly variable workloads.

- **AWS Lambda**: Follows a pay-as-you-go model, where you're charged based on the number of requests and the compute time used. It can be cost-effective for sporadic or low-traffic workloads.

• **Amazon ECS**: Costs include both container resources and the underlying EC2 instances. ECS can be cost-effective for containerized applications with consistent traffic.

• **Amazon Elastic Beanstalk**: Costs depend on the AWS resources used by your application. It's a cost-effective choice for web applications and microservices.

Making Your Decision

Ultimately, the choice of compute service depends on your specific application's requirements, workload characteristics, and your familiarity with the services. It's often a matter of finding the right balance between control, scalability, simplicity, and cost-effectiveness. AWS provides a wide range of options to accommodate a variety of use cases, so it's essential to thoroughly evaluate your needs before making a decision. Additionally, AWS offers a free tier for many services, allowing you to experiment and determine which compute service best suits your application.

Chapter 4: AWS Storage Services

Section 4.1: Amazon S3 (Simple Storage Service)

Amazon Simple Storage Service (Amazon S3) is a scalable object storage service provided by AWS. It allows you to store and retrieve data, such as files, documents, images, videos, and backups, with high durability, availability, and security. In this section, we will explore Amazon S3, its key features, and how to use it for various storage needs.

Key Features of Amazon S3:

1. Object Storage

Amazon S3 is an object storage service, meaning it stores data as objects in buckets. Each object consists of data, a unique key, and metadata. Objects can be of any size, making S3 suitable for both small files and large datasets.

2. High Durability

Amazon S3 stores data across multiple availability zones within a region to ensure high durability. Data is redundantly stored, making it highly resistant to hardware failures.

3. Availability

S3 provides high availability, allowing you to access your data from anywhere with an internet connection. It offers a service level agreement (SLA) for uptime.

4. Data Lifecycle Management

You can define data lifecycle policies to automatically transition objects to different storage classes or delete them after a specified period. This helps in cost optimization and data management.

5. Versioning

S3 supports versioning, which allows you to preserve, retrieve, and restore every version of every object stored in a bucket. This feature is valuable for data recovery and compliance.

6. Access Control

You can control access to your S3 buckets and objects using AWS Identity and Access Management (IAM) policies, bucket policies, and Access Control Lists (ACLs). This ensures that only authorized users or services can access your data.

7. Data Encryption

S3 offers data encryption both in transit and at rest. You can use server-side encryption (SSE) or client-side encryption to protect your data.

8. Event Notifications

S3 can generate event notifications when specific events occur in your buckets, such as object creation or deletion. These events can trigger actions or workflows in response.

9. Cross-Region Replication

For data redundancy and disaster recovery, you can set up cross-region replication to replicate objects from one S3 bucket to another in a different region.

10. Data Transfer Acceleration

Amazon S3 Transfer Acceleration uses Amazon CloudFront's globally distributed edge locations to accelerate uploading and downloading of objects.

Using Amazon S3:

1. Create a Bucket

To get started with Amazon S3, you need to create an S3 bucket. Buckets act as containers for storing objects. You can create buckets using the AWS Management Console, AWS CLI, or SDKs.

2. Upload Objects

Once you have a bucket, you can start uploading objects into it. Objects can be uploaded individually or in batches. You can set object permissions and metadata during the upload process.

3. Organize Objects

You can organize objects within your bucket by using prefixes (similar to directories) and naming conventions. This helps maintain a structured storage hierarchy.

4. Access Control

Implement access control policies to manage who can access your bucket and objects. Use IAM policies, bucket policies, and ACLs to define access rules.

5. Data Management

Use data lifecycle policies to automatically manage the lifecycle of objects. For example, you can move infrequently accessed data to a lower-cost storage class.

6. Data Encryption

Enable server-side encryption to protect your data at rest. You can also use client-side encryption for added security.

7. Versioning

Consider enabling versioning for critical data to maintain historical versions and protect against accidental deletions or modifications.

8. Monitor and Audit

Use Amazon S3 access logs and CloudWatch metrics to monitor and audit access to your objects. Set up event notifications to trigger actions in response to specific events.

Use Cases for Amazon S3:

1. Backup and Restore

Amazon S3 is a popular choice for backing up data and creating disaster recovery solutions. Its durability and versioning features make it suitable for data protection.

2. Static Website Hosting

You can host static websites directly from an S3 bucket, making it a cost-effective solution for web hosting.

3. Data Lakes

S3 is commonly used as a data lake for storing large volumes of structured and unstructured data for analytics and data processing.

4. Content Distribution

Combine S3 with Amazon CloudFront to distribute content globally with low latency. This is useful for serving images, videos, and other media files.

5. Data Archiving

S3 offers storage classes optimized for data archiving, making it an efficient choice for long-term data retention.

6. Application Data Storage

Many applications use S3 as a data store for user-generated content, application logs, and configuration files.

Conclusion

Amazon S3 is a versatile and highly reliable object storage service that can serve a wide range of storage needs for businesses and developers. Whether you need to store backups, host a website, build a data lake, or distribute content globally, Amazon S3 provides a scalable and secure platform for storing and retrieving data. Understanding its key features and best practices is essential for effective data management in the cloud.

Section 4.2: Amazon EBS (Elastic Block Store)

Amazon Elastic Block Store (Amazon EBS) is a block storage service offered by AWS that provides scalable and durable block-level storage volumes for use with Amazon EC2 instances. Amazon EBS volumes are designed for persistently storing data, and they are particularly useful for data that requires low-latency access. In this section, we will explore Amazon EBS, its key features, and how to use it effectively.

Key Features of Amazon EBS:

1. Block-Level Storage

Amazon EBS provides block-level storage, which means it delivers raw storage volumes that can be attached to EC2 instances. These volumes can be used like physical hard drives and are suitable for various workloads.

2. Volume Types

EBS offers several volume types optimized for different use cases: - **General Purpose (SSD)**: Provides a balance of price and performance for a wide range of workloads. - **Provisioned IOPS (SSD)**: Offers high-performance SSD volumes with configurable IOPS (Input/Output Operations Per Second). - **Throughput Optimized (HDD)**: Designed for frequently accessed, large datasets with high throughput requirements. - **Cold HDD**: Suitable for less frequently accessed data with a focus on cost savings. - **Amazon EBS-Optimized Instances**: Certain EC2 instance types are optimized for use with EBS volumes, offering dedicated bandwidth.

3. Snapshots

EBS allows you to create point-in-time snapshots of volumes. Snapshots are incremental backups that capture the changes made to data over time. You can use snapshots for data backup, recovery, and cloning volumes.

4. Encryption

EBS volumes can be encrypted using AWS Key Management Service (KMS) keys. Encryption helps protect sensitive data at rest and is a best practice for data security.

5. High Availability

EBS volumes are designed for high availability and durability. They are replicated within an Availability Zone (AZ) to protect against hardware failures.

6. Elasticity

You can easily resize EBS volumes based on your needs. This allows you to scale your storage capacity up or down as your workloads change.

7. Multi-Attach

Amazon EBS Multi-Attach is a feature that allows you to attach a single EBS volume to multiple EC2 instances simultaneously. This is useful for shared storage scenarios.

Using Amazon EBS:

1. Creating EBS Volumes

To create an EBS volume, you can use the AWS Management Console, AWS CLI, or SDKs. You specify the volume type, size, and the Availability Zone in which it should be created.

2. Attaching Volumes

Once you have created an EBS volume, you can attach it to an EC2 instance. The volume must be in the same Availability Zone as the instance. You can attach and detach volumes on-the-fly without stopping the instance.

3. Formatting and Mounting

After attaching a volume to an EC2 instance, you need to format it with a file system of your choice (e.g., ext4, NTFS) and mount it to a directory. This process varies depending on the operating system used.

4. Data Backup and Snapshots

Regularly create snapshots of your EBS volumes to back up data. Snapshots are incremental, so only changes since the last snapshot are stored, reducing storage costs.

5. Encryption

Consider enabling encryption for your EBS volumes, especially for volumes containing sensitive data. You can choose to use AWS-managed keys or your own customer-managed keys (CMKs).

6. Monitoring and Optimization

Use Amazon CloudWatch to monitor the performance of your EBS volumes. Adjust the volume type, size, or IOPS settings as needed to optimize performance.

Use Cases for Amazon EBS:

1. Boot Volumes

EBS volumes are commonly used as boot volumes for EC2 instances. The root volume of an instance is often an EBS volume, allowing for easy instance recovery and maintenance.

2. Data Storage

EBS volumes are suitable for storing application data, databases, logs, and other files that require persistent and low-latency access.

3. Backup and Recovery

Snapshots of EBS volumes are used for backup and disaster recovery purposes. You can create snapshots on a regular schedule to ensure data resilience.

4. Database Storage

Many relational database systems and NoSQL databases run on EC2 instances with EBS volumes for storing database files.

5. Shared Storage

Multi-Attach EBS volumes are used for shared storage scenarios, such as clustering, file sharing, and database replication.

Conclusion

Amazon EBS is a versatile block storage service that plays a crucial role in the storage architecture of AWS-based applications. Understanding its different volume types, snapshot capabilities, and encryption options is essential for designing reliable and performant storage solutions for your EC2 instances. Whether you need to store application data, run databases, or implement backup and recovery strategies, Amazon EBS offers the flexibility and scalability to meet your requirements.

Section 4.3: Amazon Glacier

Amazon Glacier is a low-cost archival storage service provided by AWS. It is designed for long-term data retention and archiving, making it an ideal choice for organizations looking to store data that is infrequently accessed but needs to be retained for compliance, legal, or historical purposes. In this section, we will explore Amazon Glacier, its key features, and how to use it effectively for archival storage.

Key Features of Amazon Glacier:

1. Low Cost

Amazon Glacier is cost-effective for storing large volumes of data that do not require frequent access. It offers a lower storage cost compared to other AWS storage services.

2. Data Durability

Data stored in Amazon Glacier is highly durable, with a durability rating of 99.999999999% (11 nines). This means that your data is protected against hardware failures and data corruption.

3. Data Archiving

Amazon Glacier is designed for data archiving. It is not suitable for real-time data access or frequent retrieval of data. Instead, it focuses on long-term storage.

4. Vault and Archive Structure

In Amazon Glacier, data is organized into "vaults." Each vault can contain multiple "archives." Archives are individual files or objects that you want to store in Glacier.

5. Data Retrieval Options

Retrieving data from Glacier can take several hours due to its archival nature. Amazon offers multiple retrieval options, including Expedited, Standard, and Bulk retrieval, with varying costs and retrieval times.

6. Data Encryption

Amazon Glacier encrypts your data at rest using AES-256 encryption. You can also choose to manage your own encryption keys using AWS Key Management Service (KMS).

7. Data Inventory

Amazon Glacier provides a data inventory feature that allows you to catalog and track the archives stored in your vaults. You can use this to keep records of what data you have archived.

Using Amazon Glacier:

1. Creating Vaults

To get started with Amazon Glacier, you need to create vaults to organize your archives. You can create and manage vaults using the AWS Management Console, AWS CLI, or SDKs.

2. Uploading Archives

After creating a vault, you can start uploading archives. Archives can be individual files or objects that you want to store for long-term retention. Each archive is associated with a unique archive ID.

3. Data Retrieval

Retrieving data from Amazon Glacier requires initiating a retrieval job. You specify the retrieval option (Expedited, Standard, or Bulk) and wait for the job to complete. Expedited retrieval is faster but more expensive.

4. Data Inventory

Use Amazon Glacier's data inventory feature to keep track of the archives stored in your vaults. This is particularly useful for compliance and auditing purposes.

5. Data Lifecycle Policies

You can set up data lifecycle policies to automate the transition of data from Amazon S3 to Glacier or to automate data deletion after a specified period. This helps in managing costs and compliance.

Use Cases for Amazon Glacier:

1. Compliance and Data Retention

Organizations often use Amazon Glacier to store data that must be retained for compliance or legal reasons, such as financial records, healthcare data, or legal documents.

2. Backup and Archive

Amazon Glacier is suitable for long-term data backup and archival purposes. It provides a cost-effective way to store backup copies of data that are rarely accessed.

3. Media and Entertainment

Media companies may use Glacier to archive large video and audio files, ensuring they are available for future use or reference.

4. Research and Scientific Data

Scientific institutions and research organizations use Amazon Glacier to archive research data and scientific observations for long-term preservation.

Conclusion

Amazon Glacier is an economical solution for organizations that need to archive and retain data for extended periods while minimizing storage costs. It is essential to understand Glacier's retrieval options and archival nature, as it is not suitable for real-time data access. When used appropriately, Amazon Glacier can help organizations meet compliance requirements, maintain data durability, and reduce storage expenses for archived data.

Section 4.4: Amazon EFS (Elastic File System)

Amazon Elastic File System (Amazon EFS) is a scalable and managed file storage service provided by AWS. It is designed to provide shared file storage for multiple Amazon EC2 instances, making it suitable for applications that require file sharing across instances in a scalable and highly available manner. In this section, we will explore Amazon EFS, its key features, and how to use it effectively for shared file storage.

Key Features of Amazon EFS:

1. Fully Managed

Amazon EFS is a fully managed service, meaning AWS takes care of infrastructure management, patching, and maintenance tasks. This allows you to focus on your application rather than managing file servers.

2. Scalable

EFS can automatically scale to accommodate the storage needs of your applications. You can start with a small amount of storage and grow as needed without provisioning or managing additional hardware.

3. Shared File Storage

Amazon EFS allows multiple Amazon EC2 instances to share access to a single file system. This is particularly useful for applications that require shared data among instances, such as web servers or distributed applications.

4. POSIX File System

EFS supports the Network File System version 4 (NFSv4) protocol, which makes it compatible with POSIX-compliant file systems. This compatibility ensures that your applications can work seamlessly with EFS.

5. High Availability

Amazon EFS provides high availability by replicating data across multiple Availability Zones within a region. This ensures that your data remains accessible even if one Availability Zone experiences an outage.

6. Data Encryption

Data in Amazon EFS can be encrypted both in transit and at rest. You can use AWS Key Management Service (KMS) keys to manage encryption.

7. Lifecycle Management

EFS supports lifecycle management policies that allow you to automatically move files to a lower-cost storage class as they age. This helps optimize storage costs.

Using Amazon EFS:

1. Creating File Systems

To get started with Amazon EFS, you need to create a file system. You can do this using the AWS Management Console, AWS CLI, or SDKs. During creation, you can specify the performance mode and throughput mode.

2. Mounting File Systems

Once a file system is created, you can mount it to Amazon EC2 instances. Mount points act as access points to the file system, allowing instances to read and write data. You can mount EFS file systems at boot time or manually.

3. Access Control

EFS uses POSIX permissions to control access to files and directories. You can set permissions using standard Linux file permissions or by applying Access Control Lists (ACLs).

4. Data Sharing

Multiple EC2 instances can simultaneously access the same EFS file system, making it suitable for scenarios like content sharing, data synchronization, and application data sharing.

5. Backup and Recovery

You can create backups (EFS-to-EFS backups) of your EFS file systems to protect against accidental data loss or corruption. Backups are stored in a separate EFS file system.

6. Monitoring and Performance Tuning

Use Amazon CloudWatch to monitor the performance of your EFS file systems. You can also adjust the throughput mode and bursting settings to optimize performance for your workloads.

Use Cases for Amazon EFS:

1. Web Serving

EFS is suitable for web servers that need to share static content and configuration files across multiple EC2 instances. It allows for centralized content management.

2. Content Management

Media companies and content providers can use EFS to store and share large media files, videos, and images across multiple instances, improving content delivery.

3. Data Analytics

Amazon EFS is used for storing and sharing data among multiple analytics instances, making it easier to process and analyze large datasets collaboratively.

4. DevOps and Development

Development teams can use EFS to share code repositories, build artifacts, and development environments, facilitating collaboration and version control.

Conclusion

Amazon Elastic File System (EFS) is a valuable service for applications that require shared file storage across multiple EC2 instances. It offers scalability, high availability, and ease of use, making it suitable for a wide range of use cases, from web serving to data analytics and development environments. Understanding how to create and manage EFS file systems, set up access control, and monitor performance is essential for effectively using EFS to meet your application's file storage needs.

Section 4.5: Data Backup and Recovery Strategies

Data backup and recovery are crucial aspects of any organization's IT infrastructure. Having robust strategies in place ensures that data can be protected from loss, corruption, and unauthorized access while also being recoverable in case of disasters. In this section, we will explore data backup and recovery strategies in the context of AWS, including best practices and AWS services that can help safeguard your data.

Importance of Data Backup and Recovery:

1. Data Loss Prevention

Data can be lost due to various reasons, including hardware failures, software bugs, human errors, and cyberattacks. Regular backups serve as a safety net to prevent permanent data loss.

2. Disaster Recovery

Natural disasters, such as floods, fires, or earthquakes, can disrupt data centers. Having off-site backups enables disaster recovery and ensures data availability in such scenarios.

3. Compliance and Legal Requirements

Many industries and organizations must adhere to data retention and compliance regulations. Proper backup and recovery procedures help meet these requirements.

AWS Data Backup and Recovery Services:

1. Amazon S3

Amazon S3 is a reliable storage service that can be used for data backup. You can create snapshots of your S3 buckets or replicate data across regions for redundancy. Versioning can also help recover previous versions of objects.

2. Amazon EBS Snapshots

For EC2 instances using Amazon Elastic Block Store (EBS) volumes, taking regular EBS snapshots is a common backup strategy. Snapshots capture the state of the EBS volume at a specific point in time, allowing you to restore data if needed.

3. Amazon RDS Automated Backups

Amazon Relational Database Service (RDS) offers automated daily backups of your databases, which can be retained for a specified duration. Additionally, you can create manual snapshots for on-demand backups.

4. AWS Backup

AWS Backup is a centralized service for managing backups across AWS resources. It supports various AWS services, including EC2 instances, EBS volumes, RDS databases, and more. You can set backup policies and retention periods.

Best Practices for Data Backup and Recovery on AWS:

1. Define a Backup Policy

Create a clear backup policy that outlines what data needs to be backed up, how often backups should occur, and the retention period. Ensure that this policy aligns with your organization's business and compliance requirements.

2. Use Multiple Storage Locations

Distribute backups across multiple AWS regions and Availability Zones to enhance redundancy and data durability. This mitigates the risk of data loss due to regional failures.

3. Test Backup and Recovery Procedures

Regularly test your backup and recovery procedures to ensure they work as expected. Performing test restores can uncover issues and allow you to refine your processes.

4. Automate Backup Processes

Leverage automation tools and scripts to schedule backups and enforce backup policies consistently. AWS Lambda and CloudWatch Events can be used to trigger backup tasks.

5. Encrypt Backup Data

Enable encryption for backup data, both at rest and in transit. AWS provides encryption options such as AWS Key Management Service (KMS) for managing encryption keys.

6. Monitor Backup Status

Implement monitoring and alerting for backup jobs to detect failures or issues in real-time. CloudWatch alarms can be set up to notify you of backup job status changes.

7. Document Recovery Procedures

Document the steps required to recover data from backups. Having clear and well-documented recovery procedures can significantly reduce downtime during a data loss event.

8. Establish Access Controls

Implement access controls to ensure that only authorized personnel can perform backup and recovery operations. Use AWS Identity and Access Management (IAM) to manage permissions.

Conclusion

Data backup and recovery are fundamental components of data management and disaster preparedness. In AWS, a combination of services like Amazon S3, EBS snapshots, RDS automated backups, and AWS Backup can be leveraged to implement effective backup and recovery strategies. Following best practices, defining clear policies, and regularly testing your backup and recovery procedures are essential steps to safeguard your data and ensure business continuity in the event of data loss or disasters.

Chapter 5: Networking and Content Delivery

Section 5.1: Amazon VPC (Virtual Private Cloud)

Amazon Virtual Private Cloud (Amazon VPC) is a fundamental building block of AWS infrastructure that allows you to create isolated networks within the AWS cloud. With Amazon VPC, you can control your network environment, including IP address ranges, subnets, route tables, and network gateways. In this section, we will delve into Amazon VPC, its key concepts, and how to design and configure virtual private clouds in AWS.

Key Concepts of Amazon VPC:

1. Virtual Private Cloud (VPC)

An Amazon VPC is a logically isolated section of the AWS cloud where you can launch AWS resources. It acts as your private network within the AWS environment, allowing you to define your IP address space.

2. Subnets

Subnets are subdivisions of an Amazon VPC, each associated with a specific Availability Zone (AZ). They provide network isolation within a VPC and help distribute resources across multiple AZs for high availability.

3. IP Addressing

In Amazon VPC, you have full control over IP address ranges. You can define private IPv4 addresses, public IPv4 addresses, and IPv6 addresses. Private subnets use private IPv4 addresses, while public subnets can use public IPv4 addresses.

4. Route Tables

Each subnet in an Amazon VPC is associated with a route table, which determines the traffic routing within the VPC. Route tables define how traffic is directed to the internet, other subnets, or on-premises networks.

5. Security Groups

Security groups act as virtual firewalls for Amazon EC2 instances within a VPC. They control inbound and outbound traffic at the instance level, allowing you to specify rules based on protocols, ports, and IP ranges.

6. Network Access Control Lists (NACLs)

NACLs are stateless, subnet-level network security controls. They operate at the subnet level and control traffic entering or leaving the subnet based on rules defined for inbound and outbound traffic.

7. Internet Gateway

An Internet Gateway (IGW) is a horizontally scaled, redundant, and highly available VPC component that allows communication between instances within the VPC and the internet. It is used for instances in public subnets.

8. Virtual Private Network (VPN) and Direct Connect

Amazon VPC can be connected to your on-premises data centers via VPN or AWS Direct Connect, allowing you to create a hybrid network architecture.

Designing and Configuring Amazon VPC:

1. VPC Creation

To create a VPC, you can use the AWS Management Console, AWS CLI, or CloudFormation templates. During creation, you specify the IP address range for your VPC, configure DNS settings, and set up DHCP options.

2. Subnet Configuration

Divide your VPC into subnets, taking into account your resource placement requirements and high availability needs. Allocate appropriate IP address ranges to each subnet.

3. Routing

Create route tables for your subnets, specifying routes for internet-bound traffic via the Internet Gateway or VPN/Direct Connect for on-premises access. Adjust route tables as needed.

4. Security

Implement security groups and NACLs to control inbound and outbound traffic. Define rules based on the principle of least privilege to enhance security.

5. Connectivity

Connect your VPC to the internet using an Internet Gateway if you have resources in public subnets. Establish VPN or Direct Connect connections for hybrid architectures.

6. Monitoring and Management

Utilize Amazon CloudWatch and AWS Config to monitor the health and performance of your VPC and associated resources. Regularly review and optimize your VPC configuration.

Use Cases for Amazon VPC:

1. Web Applications

Amazon VPC is commonly used for hosting web applications, allowing you to securely isolate web servers, application servers, and databases in separate subnets.

2. Enterprise Applications

Large organizations leverage VPCs to host enterprise applications, ensuring the isolation and control necessary for data security and compliance.

3. Hybrid Cloud

Amazon VPC facilitates hybrid cloud deployments, enabling seamless integration between on-premises data centers and AWS resources while maintaining network isolation.

4. Secure Data Storage

VPCs are used for storing sensitive data, such as personal or financial information, in private subnets with strict access controls.

Conclusion

Amazon Virtual Private Cloud (Amazon VPC) empowers AWS users to create and manage isolated network environments tailored to their specific requirements. Understanding the core concepts of VPC, designing robust network architectures, and implementing security measures are essential steps in building secure and scalable AWS solutions. Whether hosting web applications, enterprise systems, or hybrid cloud environments, Amazon VPC is a foundational component for achieving network isolation, security, and control within the AWS cloud.

Section 5.2: Amazon Route 53

Amazon Route 53 is a scalable and highly available Domain Name System (DNS) web service provided by AWS. It plays a critical role in connecting user requests to infrastructure running in AWS, such as EC2 instances, load balancers, and S3 buckets, as well as external resources. In this section, we will explore Amazon Route 53, its key features, and how it enables efficient DNS management and traffic routing.

Key Features of Amazon Route 53:

1. DNS Management

Amazon Route 53 allows you to register domain names and manage the DNS records for your domains. You can create, update, and delete records to control how domain names resolve to IP addresses.

2. Global Anycast Network

Route 53 operates on a global anycast network, ensuring low-latency and high-performance DNS resolution for users worldwide. It automatically routes traffic to the nearest healthy data center.

3. Traffic Routing

You can configure Route 53 to route traffic based on various routing policies, including simple routing, weighted routing, latency-based routing, geolocation routing, and failover routing. This allows you to implement load balancing and high availability.

4. Health Checks

Route 53 provides health checks to monitor the health of your resources, such as EC2 instances or load balancers. If a resource becomes unhealthy, Route 53 can automatically reroute traffic to healthy resources.

5. Alias Records

Alias records enable you to map your domain names to AWS resources without exposing underlying IP addresses. This is especially useful for routing traffic to AWS resources like S3 buckets, CloudFront distributions, and load balancers.

6. Domain Registration

Route 53 offers domain registration services, allowing you to register and manage domain names directly within the AWS ecosystem.

Using Amazon Route 53:

1. Domain Registration

To get started with Route 53, you can register domain names directly through the Route 53 console. Once registered, you can manage DNS records and configure routing policies.

2. DNS Record Management

Route 53 supports various types of DNS records, including A records, CNAME records, MX records, and more. You can create and manage these records to control how your domain names resolve to IP addresses.

3. Traffic Routing Policies

Configure traffic routing policies based on your requirements. For example, weighted routing can distribute traffic across multiple resources in different proportions, while latency-based routing directs users to the nearest endpoint.

4. Health Checks

Set up health checks to monitor the health of your resources. You can configure Route 53 to automatically fail over to healthy resources if a health check fails.

5. Alias Records

Use alias records to map domain names to AWS resources, such as an S3 bucket or a CloudFront distribution. This enables flexible and dynamic routing to AWS services.

Use Cases for Amazon Route 53:

1. Website Hosting

Route 53 is commonly used to route traffic to web servers hosted on EC2 instances or load balancers, ensuring high availability and load distribution.

2. Content Delivery

Route 53 can be integrated with Amazon CloudFront to route traffic to CloudFront distributions for efficient content delivery, including static assets and media files.

3. Disaster Recovery

Implementing failover routing policies with Route 53 helps maintain service availability in the event of resource failures or disasters.

4. Geolocation-Based Services

Geolocation routing allows businesses to provide region-specific content or services based on the user's geographical location.

Conclusion

Amazon Route 53 is a versatile DNS web service that plays a crucial role in connecting users to resources hosted in AWS. Whether you need to manage DNS records, implement traffic routing policies, or ensure high availability, Route 53 provides the tools and capabilities to support a wide range of use cases. Understanding how to configure and leverage Route 53 effectively is essential for maintaining a reliable and performant online presence in AWS.

Section 5.3: Elastic Load Balancing

Amazon Elastic Load Balancing (ELB) is a managed load balancing service provided by AWS that distributes incoming application traffic across multiple targets, such as Amazon EC2 instances, containers, and IP addresses, in one or more Availability Zones. Elastic Load Balancing helps ensure high availability, fault tolerance, and scalability for your applications. In this section, we will explore Amazon Elastic Load Balancing, its key features, and how to set up and manage load balancers in AWS.

Key Features of Amazon Elastic Load Balancing:

1. Load Balancer Types

Amazon ELB offers three types of load balancers: - **Application Load Balancer (ALB):** Best suited for routing HTTP/HTTPS traffic and provides advanced features like content-based routing, host-based routing, and WebSocket support. - **Network Load Balancer (NLB):** Ideal for handling TCP and UDP traffic with high throughput, low latency, and static IP addresses. - **Classic Load Balancer (CLB):** The original ELB type, suitable for distributing traffic across EC2 instances. CLB is being gradually replaced by ALB and NLB.

2. Health Checks

ELB performs health checks on the registered targets to determine their availability. Unhealthy targets are automatically removed from the load balancer rotation until they become healthy again.

3. Auto Scaling Integration

Elastic Load Balancing seamlessly integrates with Auto Scaling groups, allowing you to automatically scale your application based on traffic load. New instances are registered with the load balancer upon launch.

4. SSL/TLS Termination

ELB supports SSL/TLS termination, allowing it to handle encryption and decryption of traffic. This offloads the SSL/TLS processing from your application instances.

5. Cross-Zone Load Balancing

By default, ELB evenly distributes traffic across all available targets, regardless of the target's Availability Zone. This improves fault tolerance and availability.

6. Sticky Sessions

Session affinity, also known as sticky sessions, can be configured to route requests from the same client to the same target. This is useful for applications that require session persistence.

7. Content-Based Routing (ALB)

Application Load Balancers can route traffic based on content patterns in the URL path or host header. This enables advanced routing scenarios for microservices and APIs.

Setting Up Amazon Elastic Load Balancing:

1. Load Balancer Creation

To create a load balancer, you can use the AWS Management Console, AWS CLI, or CloudFormation templates. During creation, you configure the type of load balancer, listeners, and target groups.

2. Listener Configuration

Listeners define the protocol and port on which the load balancer listens for incoming traffic. You can configure multiple listeners to handle different types of traffic.

3. Target Groups

Target groups are used to route traffic to specific sets of targets, such as EC2 instances. You can define health checks, stickiness policies, and routing rules within target groups.

4. Registering Targets

Register the targets (e.g., EC2 instances) with the appropriate target group. ELB automatically distributes traffic to registered, healthy targets.

5. DNS Name Assignment

Amazon Elastic Load Balancing provides a DNS name that you can use to route traffic to the load balancer. Clients resolve the DNS name to the load balancer's IP addresses.

Use Cases for Amazon Elastic Load Balancing:

1. High Availability

Load balancing ensures that your application remains available even if some of the targets become unhealthy or experience failures.

2. Scalability

ELB supports auto scaling, enabling your application to dynamically add or remove instances based on traffic load.

3. SSL/TLS Offloading

Offloading SSL/TLS processing to the load balancer reduces the computational load on your application instances.

4. Content-Based Routing

Application Load Balancers are ideal for microservices architectures, where traffic can be routed to different services based on content patterns.

5. Fault Tolerance

By distributing traffic across multiple Availability Zones, ELB enhances fault tolerance and minimizes downtime.

Conclusion

Amazon Elastic Load Balancing (ELB) is a fundamental component for building highly available, scalable, and fault-tolerant applications in AWS. Whether you need to distribute traffic across EC2 instances, containers, or IP addresses, ELB provides the necessary load balancing capabilities. Understanding the types of load balancers, configuring listeners and target groups, and integrating ELB with Auto Scaling are essential skills for optimizing the performance and reliability of your AWS-hosted applications.

Section 5.4: Amazon CloudFront

Amazon CloudFront is a content delivery network (CDN) service provided by AWS that accelerates the distribution of web content to users worldwide. It enhances the performance, scalability, and security of web applications by caching and delivering content from edge locations closest to the end-users. In this section, we will explore Amazon CloudFront, its key features, and how to set up and optimize content delivery in AWS.

Key Features of Amazon CloudFront:

1. Global Content Distribution

CloudFront operates on a network of edge locations strategically located around the world. This enables low-latency content delivery to users regardless of their geographical location.

2. Caching

CloudFront caches content at its edge locations, reducing the load on the origin server and improving content delivery speed. You can control cache behavior using cache policies and invalidation.

3. Content Compression

CloudFront supports content compression, reducing the size of files before they are transmitted to end-users. This results in faster page load times and reduced data transfer costs.

4. Custom SSL/TLS Certificates

You can configure custom SSL/TLS certificates for your CloudFront distributions, allowing you to secure content delivery over HTTPS with your own domain name.

5. Integration with AWS Services

CloudFront integrates seamlessly with other AWS services, including S3, EC2, Lambda@Edge, and API Gateway, making it easy to serve content and APIs from your existing AWS infrastructure.

6. Security Features

CloudFront provides security features such as DDoS protection, web application firewall (WAF) integration, and field-level encryption to enhance the security of your applications.

Setting Up Amazon CloudFront:

1. Distribution Creation

To set up CloudFront, you create a distribution that specifies the origin server (e.g., an S3 bucket or a web server) from which CloudFront retrieves content. You can configure various distribution settings.

2. Cache Behavior

Define cache behaviors to control how CloudFront caches and serves content. Cache behaviors specify criteria such as path patterns and query string parameters.

3. Customization

Configure custom SSL/TLS certificates and set up custom domain names (CNAMEs) to personalize the URLs used to access your content via CloudFront.

4. Security Settings

Enable security features like DDoS protection and web application firewall (WAF) to safeguard your applications from malicious traffic.

5. Content Invalidation

When you update or remove content from your origin server, you can use cache invalidation to remove outdated content from CloudFront edge locations.

Optimizing Content Delivery:

1. Caching Strategies

Design effective caching strategies by specifying cache behaviors and TTL (Time-to-Live) values based on the nature of your content.

2. Content Compression

Enable content compression for text-based resources (e.g., HTML, CSS, JavaScript) to reduce latency and data transfer costs.

3. Regional Edge Caches

Leverage regional edge caches for frequently accessed content, optimizing delivery even further.

4. Lambda@Edge

Use AWS Lambda@Edge to execute serverless functions at CloudFront edge locations, enabling dynamic content generation and customization.

5. Origin Shield

Implement an origin shield to reduce the load on your origin server by having a centralized cache for frequently requested content.

Use Cases for Amazon CloudFront:

1. Website Acceleration

CloudFront accelerates the delivery of static and dynamic web content, resulting in faster page load times and improved user experiences.

2. Video Streaming

Video-on-demand (VOD) and live video streaming benefit from CloudFront's low-latency delivery, scalability, and global reach.

3. Software Distribution

Distribute software updates, patches, and downloadable applications efficiently to users worldwide using CloudFront's edge locations.

4. Content Personalization

CloudFront, in combination with Lambda@Edge, enables personalized content delivery based on user preferences and behavior.

5. *API Acceleration*

Accelerate the delivery of APIs and microservices by using CloudFront to cache and distribute API responses.

Conclusion

Amazon CloudFront is a powerful CDN service that plays a crucial role in improving the performance, scalability, and security of web applications and content delivery. Leveraging CloudFront's global network of edge locations, caching capabilities, and integration with AWS services can significantly enhance the user experience and reduce the operational load on your origin servers. Understanding how to set up and optimize CloudFront distributions is essential for efficient content delivery in AWS-hosted applications.

Section 5.5: Connecting On-Premises Data Centers

Amazon Web Services (AWS) provides multiple solutions for connecting on-premises data centers to the AWS cloud. Establishing these connections enables organizations to extend their existing infrastructure, migrate workloads, and build hybrid cloud environments. In this section, we will explore the various methods and services available for connecting on-premises data centers to AWS.

Key Methods for Connecting On-Premises Data Centers to AWS:

1. AWS Direct Connect

AWS Direct Connect is a dedicated network connection that provides private, low-latency access to AWS services. It bypasses the public internet, offering a secure and consistent connection between on-premises data centers and AWS regions. Direct Connect is particularly useful for applications requiring high bandwidth and predictable network performance.

2. Site-to-Site VPN

Site-to-Site Virtual Private Network (VPN) establishes an encrypted connection over the public internet between your on-premises network and an AWS Virtual Private Cloud (VPC). VPN connections are cost-effective and suitable for applications with lower bandwidth requirements.

3. AWS Transit Gateway

AWS Transit Gateway simplifies network architecture by providing a hub-and-spoke model for connecting multiple VPCs and on-premises networks. It streamlines network management and allows for consistent routing and security policies.

4. AWS Direct Connect Gateway

AWS Direct Connect Gateway extends the capabilities of AWS Direct Connect to connect multiple VPCs across different AWS regions to an on-premises data center. It simplifies network connectivity and reduces the need for multiple Direct Connect connections.

5. VPN CloudHub

VPN CloudHub enables you to establish multiple Site-to-Site VPN connections from your on-premises data center to multiple AWS VPCs. It is suitable for organizations with distributed workloads across multiple VPCs.

Setting Up Connectivity to On-Premises Data Centers:

1. AWS Direct Connect

- **Provision Direct Connect**: Create a Direct Connect connection using AWS Direct Connect partners or by colocating equipment in an AWS Direct Connect location.

- **Create Virtual Interfaces**: Configure virtual interfaces to connect to specific VPCs or to AWS services like Amazon S3.

- **BGP Configuration**: Configure Border Gateway Protocol (BGP) settings for route propagation and failover.

2. Site-to-Site VPN

- **VPN Gateway Setup**: Set up a VPN gateway in the AWS region to which you want to connect.

- **Customer Gateway**: Define a customer gateway representing your on-premises device.

- **VPN Connection**: Create a VPN connection that links the AWS VPN gateway and the customer gateway.

- **Routing Configuration**: Configure route propagation and routing tables for traffic flow.

3. AWS Transit Gateway

- **Create Transit Gateway**: Create an AWS Transit Gateway and attach your VPCs and on-premises networks.

- **Route Tables**: Configure route tables to control traffic between connected networks.

- **VPN Attachment**: Attach VPN connections or Direct Connect gateways to the Transit Gateway for hybrid connectivity.

4. AWS Direct Connect Gateway

- **Create Direct Connect Gateway**: Establish a Direct Connect Gateway and associate it with Direct Connect connections in multiple regions.

- **VPC Associations**: Associate VPCs with the Direct Connect Gateway to enable communication with on-premises networks.

- **Routing**: Set up route propagation for VPCs and on-premises networks.

5. VPN CloudHub

- **Configure VPNs**: Establish Site-to-Site VPN connections between your on-premises data center and each AWS VPC.

- **Routing Configuration**: Define routing rules to enable traffic flow between the on-premises network and VPCs.

Use Cases for Connecting On-Premises Data Centers:

1. Hybrid Cloud

Organizations can build hybrid cloud architectures by connecting on-premises data centers to AWS. This allows for seamless resource migration, disaster recovery, and scalability.

2. Data Replication and Backup

Connecting on-premises data centers to AWS facilitates data replication and backup, ensuring data redundancy and disaster recovery capabilities.

3. Cloud Bursting

Cloud bursting enables organizations to extend their on-premises resources to AWS during peak demand periods, optimizing resource utilization and cost-efficiency.

4. Compliance and Security

For industries with strict compliance requirements, connecting on-premises data centers to AWS can provide the necessary security controls and data protection mechanisms.

5. Latency-Sensitive Applications

Certain applications, such as those requiring low-latency connections to on-premises databases, benefit from Direct Connect to ensure consistent network performance.

Conclusion

Connecting on-premises data centers to AWS is a fundamental step in building hybrid cloud solutions and optimizing resource utilization. AWS offers a range of connectivity options, from AWS Direct Connect to Site-to-Site VPNs and Transit Gateway, allowing organizations to choose the method that best fits their requirements. Understanding the setup and configuration of these connections is essential for creating robust and efficient hybrid cloud environments.

You've got the list of all the chapters of the book. If you need any information or content from a specific chapter, please let me know, and I'll be happy to provide it for you.

Chapter 6: Database Services on AWS

Section 6.1: Amazon RDS (Relational Database Service)

Amazon RDS (Relational Database Service) is a managed database service offered by AWS that simplifies the setup, operation, and scaling of relational databases. It supports popular database engines like MySQL, PostgreSQL, MariaDB, Oracle, and Microsoft SQL Server. Amazon RDS is designed to handle routine database tasks, allowing you to focus on your application's development rather than database administration. In this section, we'll delve into Amazon RDS, its features, supported database engines, and how to get started with it.

Key Features of Amazon RDS:

1. Managed Service

Amazon RDS automates database tasks such as patching, backups, and software updates. AWS manages the infrastructure, freeing you from many administrative burdens.

2. Multi-AZ Deployments

You can configure Amazon RDS for high availability with Multi-AZ deployments, which replicate your database across multiple Availability Zones. This ensures database availability even in the event of hardware failures or maintenance activities.

3. Automated Backups

Amazon RDS automatically takes daily backups of your database and retains them for a specified retention period. You can restore your database to any point in time within this window.

4. Scaling Resources

Easily scale your database resources up or down to accommodate changing workloads. Amazon RDS supports vertical scaling (CPU and RAM) and read replicas for horizontal scaling.

5. Security Features

Amazon RDS offers security features such as network isolation with Amazon VPC, encryption at rest and in transit, and IAM database authentication for fine-grained access control.

6. Database Engines

Supports various database engines, including MySQL, PostgreSQL, MariaDB, Oracle, and Microsoft SQL Server, allowing you to choose the one that best fits your application's requirements.

Getting Started with Amazon RDS:

1. Database Engine Selection

Select the database engine that suits your application's needs. If you're migrating an existing database, choose the engine compatible with your current database.

2. Instance Creation

Create an RDS instance specifying the instance class, storage, and other configuration settings. You can also enable Multi-AZ deployment during this setup.

3. Database Creation

After the instance is created, you can create one or more databases within it. Configure database options like character sets, collation, and encryption.

4. Security Settings

Set up security groups and configure network settings to control inbound and outbound traffic to your RDS instance. Enable encryption for enhanced security.

5. Backups and Maintenance

Configure automated backups and define a backup retention period. You can also set up maintenance windows to specify when RDS can perform maintenance tasks.

Connecting to Amazon RDS:

You can connect to your Amazon RDS instance using standard database connection libraries and tools. Obtain the endpoint and credentials from the RDS console, and use them in your application or client software.

```python
import pymysql
# RDS endpoint and credentials
```

```
db_endpoint                                          =
"your-db-instance.c3hgv2r1dpnf.us-east-1.rds.amazonaws.com"
    db_username = "your-username"
    db_password = "your-password"
    db_name = "your-database-name"
    # Create a database connection
    conn = pymysql.connect(
    host=db_endpoint,
    user=db_username,
    password=db_password,
    database=db_name,
    connect_timeout=5,
    )
    # Create a cursor
    cursor = conn.cursor()
    # Execute SQL queries
    cursor.execute("SELECT * FROM your_table")
    result = cursor.fetchall()
    # Close the cursor and connection
    cursor.close()
    conn.close()
```

Use Cases for Amazon RDS:

1. Web Applications

Amazon RDS is well-suited for web applications that require a relational database to store data, user profiles, and transaction records.

2. E-Commerce Platforms

E-commerce websites benefit from the scalability and high availability of Amazon RDS to handle product catalogs, orders, and customer data.

3. Business Applications

Business applications like CRM and ERP systems can leverage Amazon RDS for efficient data storage and management.

4. Reporting and Analytics

By creating read replicas, you can offload reporting and analytics workloads from the primary database, ensuring optimal performance.

5. Content Management Systems

CMS platforms can use Amazon RDS to store content, user accounts, and configurations.

Conclusion

Amazon RDS simplifies database management and maintenance, making it an ideal choice for applications that rely on relational databases. Its managed nature, high availability options, and support for various database engines make it a versatile and reliable solution for a wide range of use cases. Understanding how to create and configure Amazon RDS instances is crucial for effectively managing your application's database layer on AWS.

Section 6.2: Amazon DynamoDB

Amazon DynamoDB is a fully managed NoSQL database service provided by AWS. It is designed to provide high performance, scalability, and low-latency access to data, making it an excellent choice for applications that require flexible and seamless storage solutions. In this section, we will explore the features, data model, and best practices for using Amazon DynamoDB.

Key Features of Amazon DynamoDB:

1. Fully Managed

Amazon DynamoDB is a serverless, fully managed service, which means AWS handles all the administrative tasks, including hardware provisioning, configuration, software patching, and automatic scaling. You can focus solely on your application's logic.

2. NoSQL Database

DynamoDB is a NoSQL database, which allows for flexible data models. You can store structured, semi-structured, or unstructured data without the need for a fixed schema.

3. Performance at Scale

DynamoDB automatically scales to handle high traffic loads and provides low-latency access to data, making it suitable for applications with rapidly changing workloads.

4. Encryption and Security

Data at rest and in transit is encrypted by default. IAM policies and fine-grained access control enable you to restrict who can access your data.

5. Global Tables

Amazon DynamoDB Global Tables allow you to replicate your data across multiple AWS regions for high availability and fault tolerance. This feature ensures that your application remains accessible even in the event of a regional outage.

Data Model:

DynamoDB uses a schemaless data model where data is organized into tables, items, and attributes:

- **Table**: A table is a collection of items that share the same data structure. Each table must have a primary key, which can be composed of one or two attributes: the partition key and an optional sort key.

- **Item**: An item is a single data record in a table. Items are similar to rows in a traditional relational database but can have different attributes.

- **Attribute**: An attribute is a named piece of data that represents a characteristic of the item. Each item can have multiple attributes.

Creating and Querying Tables:

You can create DynamoDB tables using the AWS Management Console, AWS Command Line Interface (CLI), or an AWS SDK. When designing your tables, consider your application's access patterns, as DynamoDB is optimized for specific query patterns.

Here's an example of creating a DynamoDB table using the AWS CLI:

```
aws dynamodb create-table \
—table-name MyTable \
—attribute-definitions \
AttributeName=UserId,AttributeType=S \
AttributeName=Timestamp,AttributeType=N \
—key-schema \
AttributeName=UserId,KeyType=HASH \
AttributeName=Timestamp,KeyType=RANGE \
—provisioned-throughput \
ReadCapacityUnits=5,WriteCapacityUnits=5
```

To query data from a DynamoDB table, you can use the Query operation to retrieve items based on the table's primary key or secondary indexes. Here's a Python example using the AWS SDK for Python (Boto3):

```python
import boto3
# Initialize DynamoDB client
dynamodb = boto3.client('dynamodb')
# Define the query parameters
table_name = 'MyTable'
query_params = {
'TableName': table_name,
'KeyConditionExpression': 'UserId = :user_id',
'ExpressionAttributeValues': {':user_id': {'S': 'user123'}}
}
# Perform the query
```

```
response = dynamodb.query(**query_params)
# Retrieve the queried items
items = response['Items']
```

Best Practices:

1. **Design for Query Patterns**: Design your tables and primary keys to support your application's query patterns.
2. **Use Indexes**: Utilize secondary indexes to enable efficient querying on non-primary key attributes.
3. **Provisioned Throughput**: Set appropriate read and write capacity units based on your application's workload. DynamoDB can automatically scale throughput as needed.
4. **Use Global Tables**: If high availability across multiple regions is required, enable Global Tables.
5. **Batch Operations**: Use batch operations for efficiency when working with multiple items.
6. **Consistent Reads**: Choose between eventually consistent and strongly consistent reads based on your application's requirements.
7. **Monitor and Optimize**: Use DynamoDB's monitoring and logging features to optimize performance and cost.

Conclusion:

Amazon DynamoDB is a powerful and scalable NoSQL database service offered by AWS. Its fully managed nature, flexible data model, and high availability features make it a valuable tool for modern application development. Understanding its data model, query capabilities, and best practices is essential for building efficient and resilient applications on AWS.

Section 6.3: Amazon Redshift

Amazon Redshift is a fully managed, petabyte-scale data warehousing service provided by AWS. It is designed for high-performance data analytics and reporting. In this section, we will explore the features, architecture, and use cases of Amazon Redshift.

Key Features of Amazon Redshift:

1. Columnar Storage

Amazon Redshift stores data in a columnar format, which is optimized for analytical queries. This design improves query performance by reducing I/O and disk storage requirements.

2. Massively Parallel Processing (MPP)

Redshift employs MPP architecture, allowing it to distribute query workloads across multiple nodes for parallel execution. This results in fast query response times, even for large datasets.

3. Data Compression

Redshift uses advanced data compression techniques to reduce storage costs and improve query performance. Data is compressed and encoded efficiently during ingestion.

4. Integration with AWS Ecosystem

Amazon Redshift seamlessly integrates with other AWS services, such as Amazon S3 for data storage, AWS Glue for data preparation, and AWS Quicksight for visualization.

5. Scalability

Redshift allows you to scale your data warehouse up or down as needed, making it suitable for both small and large-scale data analytics.

6. Security and Encryption

Data in Amazon Redshift can be encrypted at rest and in transit. It supports IAM authentication and integrates with AWS Key Management Service (KMS) for key management.

Data Warehousing Architecture:

Amazon Redshift follows a data warehousing architecture with the following components:

1. Cluster

A Redshift cluster is the core infrastructure component, consisting of leader nodes and multiple compute nodes. The leader node manages query coordination, while compute nodes store and process data.

2. Data Warehouse

The data warehouse is the logical container that holds your data. It consists of one or more databases, schemas, tables, and views.

3. Node Types

Redshift offers different node types, including dense compute nodes for high performance and dense storage nodes for large storage capacity. You can choose the node type that best fits your requirements.

Use Cases for Amazon Redshift:

Amazon Redshift is well-suited for a variety of data analytics and reporting use cases, including:

1. **Business Intelligence (BI):** Redshift can power BI tools for generating reports and dashboards, enabling data-driven decision-making.
2. **Data Warehousing:** It is an ideal solution for consolidating data from various sources into a single repository for analysis.
3. **Log and Event Data Analysis:** Analyzing large volumes of log data, such as website logs or application logs, to gain insights and troubleshoot issues.
4. **Market Research:** Redshift can process large datasets for market research and trend analysis.
5. **Predictive Analytics:** Running complex queries to build predictive models and analyze historical data for future predictions.

Querying Data in Amazon Redshift:

You can query data in Redshift using standard SQL. Here's a simple example of running a query:

```sql
SELECT product_category, SUM(sales_amount)
FROM sales
WHERE order_date >= '2023-01-01'
GROUP BY product_category
ORDER BY SUM(sales_amount) DESC;
```

Loading Data into Amazon Redshift:

To load data into Redshift, you can use various methods, including:

- **Amazon S3:** You can copy data from Amazon S3 into Redshift using the COPY command.

- **AWS Glue:** Use AWS Glue for ETL (Extract, Transform, Load) jobs to prepare and load data into Redshift.

- **Data Pipeline:** AWS Data Pipeline can automate data movement and transformation tasks.

Conclusion:

Amazon Redshift is a powerful data warehousing solution that enables organizations to perform advanced data analytics and reporting at scale. Its architecture, scalability, and integration with the AWS ecosystem make it a valuable tool for businesses looking to gain insights from their data. Understanding how to design, load, and query data in Amazon Redshift is crucial for maximizing its benefits in your analytics projects.

Section 6.4: Amazon Aurora

Amazon Aurora is a high-performance, fully managed relational database service offered by AWS. It is compatible with MySQL and PostgreSQL and is designed to provide the speed and reliability of high-end commercial databases at a fraction of the cost. In this section, we will explore the key features, architecture, and benefits of Amazon Aurora.

Key Features of Amazon Aurora:

1. Compatibility

Amazon Aurora is compatible with MySQL and PostgreSQL, which means you can use familiar tools, drivers, and applications with it. You can migrate your existing MySQL or PostgreSQL databases to Aurora with minimal effort.

2. Performance

Aurora is designed for high performance. It uses a distributed, log-structured storage system that provides low-latency access to data. It also offers read replicas for read scalability.

3. Scalability

Aurora can automatically scale both read and write operations to handle high traffic loads. It supports up to 15 read replicas and can adjust its capacity based on workload.

4. Data Durability

Aurora replicates data to multiple Availability Zones (AZs) and continuously backs up your data to Amazon S3. This architecture provides data durability and fault tolerance.

5. Security

Aurora offers security features such as encryption at rest and in transit, IAM database authentication, and integration with AWS Key Management Service (KMS) for key management.

Amazon Aurora Architecture:

Amazon Aurora uses a unique architecture that separates compute and storage, resulting in high performance and scalability. The key components of Aurora's architecture include:

1. Cluster

An Aurora cluster consists of a primary instance and up to 15 read replicas. The primary instance handles write operations, while read replicas handle read operations.

2. Storage Volume

Aurora's storage volume is distributed across many disks in a distributed cluster volume. This distributed, log-structured storage allows for high performance and fault tolerance.

3. Endpoints

Aurora provides two types of endpoints: cluster endpoint and reader endpoint. The cluster endpoint is used for write operations, while the reader endpoint routes read queries to the appropriate read replicas, distributing the read workload.

Benefits of Amazon Aurora:

1. **High Performance:** Aurora offers faster read/write operations and is designed for high throughput and low latency.
2. **Compatibility:** It is compatible with MySQL and PostgreSQL, making it easy to migrate existing databases.
3. **Scalability:** Aurora can automatically scale to handle

growing workloads without manual intervention.

4. **Fault Tolerance:** Data is replicated across multiple AZs, providing high availability and durability.

5. **Security:** Aurora offers robust security features, including encryption and IAM database authentication.

6. **Cost-Effective:** Compared to traditional commercial databases, Aurora is cost-effective, offering enterprise-grade features at a lower cost.

Connecting to Amazon Aurora:

You can connect to an Amazon Aurora database using standard MySQL or PostgreSQL clients. Here's an example of connecting to an Aurora MySQL database using Python and the mysql-connector-python library:

```python
import mysql.connector
# Create a connection to the Aurora database
conn = mysql.connector.connect(
host='mydbcluster.cluster-identifier.us-east-1.rds.amazonaws.com',
user='username',
password='password',
database='mydb'
)
# Create a cursor to execute SQL queries
cursor = conn.cursor()
# Execute a query
cursor.execute('SELECT * FROM mytable')
# Fetch and print the results
results = cursor.fetchall()
for row in results:
print(row)
# Close the cursor and connection
cursor.close()
```

    conn.close()

Conclusion:

Amazon Aurora is a powerful and cost-effective relational database service that combines the best features of MySQL and PostgreSQL with the benefits of AWS cloud services. Its high performance, scalability, and compatibility make it a popular choice for applications that require a relational database backend. Understanding its architecture and how to connect to and use Amazon Aurora is essential for building efficient and reliable database solutions on AWS.

Section 6.5: Choosing the Right Database Solution

Selecting the appropriate database solution is a critical decision when architecting applications on AWS. Each database service offered by AWS has its unique characteristics, use cases, and trade-offs. In this section, we will discuss factors to consider and best practices for choosing the right database solution for your specific needs.

Factors to Consider:

1. Data Model

Consider the type of data your application manages. Is it structured (e.g., relational data) or unstructured (e.g., NoSQL data)? Choose a database that aligns with your data model.

2. Scale Requirements

Assess the scalability needs of your application. Some databases, like Amazon Aurora and Amazon RDS, offer easy scalability, while others, like Amazon DynamoDB, are designed for seamless horizontal scaling.

3. Performance

Evaluate the expected query and transactional performance of your application. High-performance workloads may benefit from services like Amazon Redshift or Amazon Elasticsearch.

4. Availability and Fault Tolerance

Consider your application's uptime requirements. Services like Amazon RDS and Amazon Aurora provide high availability and fault tolerance features, while others may require manual setup for redundancy.

5. Data Consistency

Determine the level of data consistency your application needs. Some NoSQL databases offer eventual consistency, while relational databases provide strong consistency.

6. Cost

Analyze the cost implications of your database choice, including licensing fees, storage costs, and operational overhead. AWS provides various pricing models to match your budget.

7. Managed vs. Self-Managed

Decide whether you want to manage the database yourself or use a fully managed service. AWS offers both options, but managed services reduce operational burden.

Common AWS Database Services:

1. Amazon RDS (Relational Database Service)

Amazon RDS supports relational databases like MySQL, PostgreSQL, SQL Server, and Oracle. It offers managed database instances, automatic backups, and high availability options.

2. Amazon Aurora

Amazon Aurora is a high-performance, MySQL, and PostgreSQL-compatible relational database service. It combines the benefits of open-source databases with the power of AWS.

3. Amazon DynamoDB

Amazon DynamoDB is a managed NoSQL database service that provides seamless scalability and low-latency access for applications with variable workloads.

4. Amazon Redshift

Amazon Redshift is a data warehousing service for analytics and reporting. It is optimized for high-performance, columnar storage, and complex queries.

5. *Amazon Elasticsearch Service*

Amazon Elasticsearch Service is a fully managed service for Elasticsearch, ideal for real-time log and event data analysis.

6. *Amazon DocumentDB*

Amazon DocumentDB is a managed NoSQL database compatible with MongoDB, designed for applications requiring a document database.

Best Practices for Database Selection:

1. **Understand Your Data:** Start by understanding your data's structure, volume, and access patterns.
2. **Performance Testing:** Perform performance tests to ensure your chosen database meets your application's requirements.
3. **Scalability Planning:** Plan for future growth by choosing a database that can scale with your application's needs.
4. **Cost Analysis:** Estimate the total cost of ownership, including licensing, storage, and operational expenses.
5. **High Availability:** Prioritize high availability and fault tolerance to minimize downtime.
6. **Security:** Implement security measures appropriate for your database choice, including encryption and access controls.
7. **Backup and Recovery:** Set up regular backups and define recovery procedures.
8. **Monitoring and Optimization:** Use AWS monitoring tools like Amazon CloudWatch to monitor database performance and optimize as needed.

Conclusion:

Selecting the right database solution is a crucial step in designing robust and scalable applications on AWS. By considering factors such as data model, scalability, performance, availability, cost, and management preferences, you can make an informed decision that aligns with your application's specific needs. AWS offers a wide range of database services, each tailored to different use cases, ensuring that you can find the perfect fit for your project.

Chapter 7: AWS Security and Compliance

Section 7.1: Identity and Access Management (IAM) Policies

Identity and Access Management (IAM) is a fundamental component of AWS security, allowing you to control access to your AWS resources. IAM policies define permissions, specifying what actions are allowed or denied on which resources by which entities (users, groups, roles, or AWS services). In this section, we will delve into IAM policies, their structure, and best practices for managing access control in AWS.

IAM Policy Structure:

IAM policies consist of one or more statements. Each statement has the following elements:

- **Effect:** Specifies whether the statement allows or denies access ("Allow" or "Deny").

- **Action:** Describes the AWS actions (API operations) that the policy allows or denies.

- **Resource:** Identifies the AWS resources to which the policy applies (e.g., an S3 bucket, an EC2 instance, etc.).

- **Condition:** Optionally defines conditions under which the statement is in effect. For example, time-based conditions can restrict access during specific hours.

Here's a basic IAM policy JSON structure:

```
{
"Version": "2012-10-17",
"Statement": [
{
"Effect": "Allow",
"Action": "s3:GetObject",
"Resource": "arn:aws:s3:::example-bucket/*",
"Condition": {
"IpAddress": {
"aws:SourceIp": "203.0.113.0/24"
}
}
}
]
}
```

In this example, the policy allows the "s3:GetObject" action on objects in the example-bucket only if the source IP address is within the specified range.

IAM Policy Best Practices:

1. **Least Privilege:** Apply the principle of least privilege, granting only the permissions necessary for each user or role to perform their tasks.
2. **Use IAM Roles:** Assign roles to AWS resources like EC2 instances instead of using long-term access keys for enhanced security.
3. **Regularly Review Policies:** Periodically review and audit IAM policies to ensure they remain aligned with your organization's security requirements.
4. **Enable MFA:** Require multi-factor authentication (MFA) for users who have access to sensitive resources or actions.
5. **Use IAM Groups:** Group users with similar access

requirements into IAM groups to simplify policy management.

6. **Policy Conditions:** Use conditions in policies to add fine-grained control. For example, you can restrict access based on IP address, time, or request source.

7. **Explicit Deny:** Avoid using "Deny" policies except when necessary. Explicit "Deny" statements can override "Allow" statements.

8. **Policy Versioning:** Consider versioning IAM policies to maintain a history of policy changes.

Testing IAM Policies:

You can use the IAM Policy Simulator in the AWS Management Console to test IAM policies without affecting real resources. This helps ensure that your policies grant the desired permissions and deny unauthorized access.

Policy Attachments:

IAM policies can be attached to users, groups, or roles. Users inherit permissions from the policies attached directly to them and from group memberships. Roles, on the other hand, are assumed by AWS services or federated users, allowing them to temporarily assume the permissions associated with the role.

IAM Policy Example:

Here's an example of an IAM policy that grants read-only access to an S3 bucket and write access to a specific DynamoDB table:

```
{
"Version": "2012-10-17",
"Statement": [
{
```

```
"Effect": "Allow",
"Action": "s3:GetObject",
"Resource": "arn:aws:s3:::my-bucket/*"
},
{
"Effect": "Allow",
"Action": "dynamodb:PutItem",
"Resource":
"arn:aws:dynamodb:us-east-1:123456789012:table/MyTable"
}
]
}
```

In this policy, users with this policy attached can read objects from the my-bucket S3 bucket and put items into the MyTable DynamoDB table.

Conclusion:

IAM policies are a cornerstone of AWS security, enabling fine-grained access control to AWS resources. By understanding IAM policy structure, best practices, and how to test policies, you can effectively manage access to your AWS environment while adhering to security and compliance requirements. Implementing least privilege access and regularly reviewing and optimizing your policies are crucial steps in maintaining a secure AWS environment.

Section 7.2: Security Groups and NACLs

In AWS, Security Groups and Network Access Control Lists (NACLs) are two essential tools for controlling network traffic to and from your AWS resources. They provide different levels of control and granularity in managing the security of your virtual private cloud (VPC). In this section, we will explore the concepts of

Security Groups and NACLs, how they work, and best practices for using them effectively.

Security Groups:

Security Groups (SGs) act as virtual firewalls for your EC2 instances, controlling inbound and outbound traffic at the instance level. Each EC2 instance can be associated with one or more Security Groups. Here are some key points about Security Groups:

- **Stateful:** Security Groups are stateful, which means if you allow incoming traffic from a specific IP, the corresponding outbound response traffic is automatically allowed.

- **Rule Evaluation:** Rules in Security Groups are evaluated based on the "most specific rule wins" principle. If there is no rule explicitly allowing traffic, it's denied by default.

- **Default Deny:** By default, all inbound traffic is denied unless you specify rules to allow it.

- **Instance-Level:** Security Groups are associated with individual instances, allowing you to apply different rules to different instances.

- **VPC Boundaries:** Security Groups can span multiple availability zones within a VPC.

Here's an example of a Security Group rule allowing SSH access (port 22):

```
{
    "Description": "Allow SSH access from a specific IP range",
```

```
"IpProtocol": "tcp",
"FromPort": 22,
"ToPort": 22,
"CidrIp": "203.0.113.0/24"
}
```

Network Access Control Lists (NACLs):

Network Access Control Lists (NACLs) operate at the subnet level and provide a coarse-grained control over inbound and outbound traffic. Unlike Security Groups, NACLs are stateless, meaning that if you allow incoming traffic, you must explicitly allow the corresponding outbound response traffic. Key points about NACLs include:

- **Rule Evaluation:** Rules in NACLs are evaluated in a rule number order. Lower-numbered rules are evaluated before higher-numbered rules.

- **Default Deny:** By default, all inbound and outbound traffic is denied unless you specify rules to allow it.

- **Subnet-Level:** NACLs are associated with subnets in your VPC, applying rules to all resources in that subnet.

- **VPC Boundaries:** NACLs are bound to a specific VPC and do not span multiple VPCs.

Here's an example of an inbound NACL rule allowing HTTP traffic (port 80):

```
{
"RuleNumber": 100,
"Protocol": "6",
"RuleAction": "allow",
```

```
"CidrBlock": "0.0.0.0/0",
"Egress": false,
"PortRange": {
"From": 80,
"To": 80
}
}
```

Best Practices:

1. **Layered Defense:** Use Security Groups and NACLs together to create a layered defense strategy. Security Groups provide instance-level control, while NACLs offer subnet-level control.

2. **Least Privilege:** Follow the principle of least privilege when configuring rules. Only allow the necessary traffic and deny all other traffic.

3. **Default Deny:** Always start with a default-deny rule and then add specific allow rules as needed.

4. **Regular Auditing:** Regularly audit your Security Groups and NACL rules to ensure they are up to date and adhere to your security policies.

5. **Logging and Monitoring:** Enable VPC Flow Logs to capture network traffic for analysis and monitoring. Use CloudWatch Logs to centralize and analyze logs.

6. **Documentation:** Document your Security Groups and NACL configurations, including the purpose of each rule.

7. **Backup Rules:** Make backup copies of your rule configurations to quickly restore them if needed.

Conclusion:

Security Groups and Network Access Control Lists are essential components of AWS VPC security. By understanding their differences, capabilities, and best practices, you can effectively design and manage the network security of your AWS resources, ensuring that only authorized traffic is allowed while maintaining the confidentiality and integrity of your data.

Section 7.3: AWS Inspector and Trusted Advisor

AWS Inspector and AWS Trusted Advisor are two valuable services provided by Amazon Web Services (AWS) to enhance the security and efficiency of your AWS environment. In this section, we will explore both services, their functionalities, and how they can help you maintain a secure and optimized AWS infrastructure.

AWS Inspector:

AWS Inspector is a security assessment service that helps you identify security vulnerabilities and compliance issues within your AWS resources. It achieves this by analyzing your AWS instances and applications to provide detailed findings and recommendations. Here are some key features and functionalities of AWS Inspector:

1. **Agent-Based Scanning:** AWS Inspector uses an agent that you install on your EC2 instances. This agent collects data about your instance and sends it securely to AWS for analysis.

2. **Assessment Templates:** You can create customized assessment templates specifying the rules packages and duration of assessments. AWS Inspector then performs assessments based on your defined templates.

3. **Findings and Recommendations:** After an assessment, Inspector provides findings categorized as high, medium, or low severity. It also offers recommendations on how to remediate the identified issues.

4. **Integration with AWS Config:** AWS Inspector can be integrated with AWS Config to provide continuous security monitoring and automated assessments.

5. **Compliance Standards:** AWS Inspector supports various compliance standards, including CIS benchmarks and AWS-specific best practices.

Here's an example of how you can use AWS Inspector to assess the security of your EC2 instances:

```
# Install the AWS Inspector agent on your EC2 instance
sudo curl -O https://d1wk0tztpsntt1.cloudfront.net/linux/latest/install
sudo bash install
# Create an assessment template
aws inspector create-assessment-template \
—assessment-target-arn
arn:aws:inspector:us-east-1:123456789012:target/0-0kFIPusq \
—assessment-template-name "MyAssessmentTemplate" \
—duration-in-seconds 3600 \
—rules-package-arns
arn:aws:inspector:us-east-1:758058086616:rulespackage/0-9hgA516p
```

AWS Trusted Advisor:

AWS Trusted Advisor is a service that provides real-time guidance to help you optimize your AWS infrastructure in various aspects, including cost, security, performance, and fault tolerance. It offers checks and recommendations based on AWS best practices. Key features and functionalities of AWS Trusted Advisor include:

1. **Cost Optimization:** Trusted Advisor identifies opportunities to reduce costs, such as by terminating idle instances, resizing resources, or leveraging reserved instances.
2. **Security:** It offers checks for security best practices, such as enabling multi-factor authentication (MFA) and closing security group ports that are publicly accessible.
3. **Performance:** Trusted Advisor assesses the performance of your resources and offers recommendations to improve it.
4. **Fault Tolerance:** It provides checks related to fault tolerance, such as suggesting the use of Amazon RDS Multi-AZ deployments for database redundancy.
5. **Integration with AWS Support Plans:** AWS Trusted Advisor comes with varying levels of access based on your AWS Support plan. Higher-level plans offer more checks and recommendations.

Here's an example of how you can use AWS Trusted Advisor to check for security-related recommendations:

```
# List security checks and their statuses
aws support describe-trusted-advisor-checks \
—language en \
—category "security"
```

Conclusion:

AWS Inspector and Trusted Advisor are valuable tools for improving the security and efficiency of your AWS environment. Inspector helps you identify and remediate security vulnerabilities and compliance issues, while Trusted Advisor offers real-time guidance to optimize various aspects of your AWS infrastructure. By regularly using these services, you can maintain a more secure, cost-effective, and performant AWS environment while adhering to best practices and industry standards.

Section 7.4: Encryption and Key Management

Encryption is a fundamental security practice that protects data at rest and in transit by converting it into an unreadable format unless you possess the appropriate decryption key. AWS provides various services and tools for encrypting data and managing encryption keys, ensuring the confidentiality and integrity of your sensitive information.

Data Encryption at Rest:

AWS offers several services that automatically encrypt data at rest, providing a robust layer of protection for your stored data:

1. **Amazon S3 Encryption:** Amazon S3 supports server-side encryption (SSE) for objects stored in S3 buckets. SSE can use AWS-managed keys (SSE-S3), customer-provided keys (SSE-C), or AWS Key Management Service (KMS) keys (SSE-KMS).

2. **Amazon EBS Encryption:** Amazon Elastic Block Store (EBS) volumes can be encrypted using AWS-managed keys or customer-provided keys. When enabled, all data stored on the EBS volume is encrypted.

3. **Amazon RDS Encryption:** Amazon Relational Database Service (RDS) supports encryption of database instances, including both the data and the automated backups. You can use either AWS-managed keys or your own KMS keys.

4. **Amazon EFS Encryption:** Amazon Elastic File System (EFS) supports encryption of data at rest. It uses a customer-managed key stored in AWS KMS for encryption.

Data Encryption in Transit:

Encrypting data in transit ensures that data transmitted between AWS services, resources, or clients is protected. AWS provides encryption mechanisms for various services:

1. **SSL/TLS:** Many AWS services, including Amazon RDS, Amazon Redshift, and Amazon CloudFront, use SSL/TLS encryption to secure data in transit. You can enable SSL/TLS for services that support it.
2. **Amazon VPC Peering:** Traffic between Amazon VPCs across a VPC peering connection is encrypted by default.
3. **Direct Connect:** AWS Direct Connect connections can be configured to use SSL/TLS encryption to secure data as it traverses the connection.

AWS Key Management Service (KMS):

AWS KMS is a managed service that simplifies the creation and control of encryption keys. Here are some key features and functionalities of AWS KMS:

1. **Key Creation:** KMS allows you to create and manage cryptographic keys that can be used for data encryption and decryption.
2. **Integration:** Many AWS services integrate seamlessly with KMS for encryption purposes. For example, you can use KMS keys to encrypt S3 objects, RDS instances, and more.
3. **Key Rotation:** KMS supports automatic key rotation to

enhance security by regularly replacing cryptographic material.

4. **Audit Trails:** KMS provides audit trails and logs for key usage, allowing you to monitor and trace access to your encryption keys.

5. **Granular Access Control:** You can define fine-grained access control policies for your keys, specifying which IAM users or roles can use them.

Here's an example of creating an AWS KMS key:

 # Create a symmetric KMS key

aws kms create-key—description "MyEncryptionKey"

Best Practices:

1. **Use Encryption by Default:** Enable encryption for data at rest and in transit wherever possible, especially for sensitive information.

2. **Rotate Keys Regularly:** Implement key rotation for sensitive keys to minimize the exposure of cryptographic material.

3. **Manage Key Access:** Restrict access to encryption keys to only those entities that require it, using IAM policies.

4. **Monitor Key Usage:** Use AWS CloudTrail to monitor key usage and keep track of who is accessing your keys.

5. **Secure Key Storage:** Safeguard your encryption keys, as they are critical for data security. AWS KMS offers hardware security modules (HSMs) for added protection.

6. **Keep Abreast of Updates:** Stay informed about AWS updates and improvements related to encryption to ensure your encryption practices remain effective and up-to-date.

Encryption and key management are vital components of a comprehensive security strategy in AWS. By implementing strong encryption practices and leveraging AWS KMS for key management, you can protect your data from unauthorized access and ensure the security and compliance of your AWS environment.

Section 7.5: Compliance Frameworks

Compliance frameworks provide guidelines and best practices for achieving and maintaining compliance with specific regulatory requirements or industry standards. AWS offers a range of tools, services, and resources to help you meet the compliance requirements of various frameworks. In this section, we'll explore some of the prominent compliance frameworks supported by AWS and how you can use AWS services to achieve compliance.

Key Compliance Frameworks:

1. HIPAA (Health Insurance Portability and Accountability Act):

- **AWS HIPAA Compliance:** AWS provides a HIPAA compliance program that covers services in the AWS environment. AWS services like Amazon RDS, Amazon S3, and AWS Identity and Access Management (IAM) can be used in HIPAA-compliant solutions.

- **Business Associate Addendum (BAA):** AWS offers a BAA that outlines AWS's responsibilities for HIPAA compliance and provides assurance that AWS will maintain the security and confidentiality of protected health information (PHI).

- **Encryption and Access Control:** Implement encryption of PHI at rest and in transit, and apply strict access control policies to protect patient data.

2. PCI DSS (Payment Card Industry Data Security Standard):

- **AWS PCI Compliance:** AWS complies with PCI DSS requirements and offers services that help you build PCI-compliant applications. AWS provides guidance on securing cardholder data environments (CDEs) and maintaining compliance.

- **Tokenization and Encryption:** AWS Key Management Service (KMS) can be used for encryption and tokenization of sensitive cardholder data.

- **Security Groups and Network ACLs:** Use AWS security groups and network ACLs to control inbound and outbound traffic to and from your CDE.

3. FedRAMP (Federal Risk and Authorization Management Program):

- **AWS FedRAMP Compliance:** AWS offers a range of services that comply with FedRAMP requirements, enabling government agencies to leverage AWS for their workloads.

- **FedRAMP Moderate and High Baselines:** AWS provides services that meet the FedRAMP Moderate and High baselines, allowing government agencies to deploy sensitive workloads in the cloud.

- **AWS GovCloud (US):** AWS GovCloud (US) is designed to host sensitive data and regulated workloads for U.S. government agencies and contractors, ensuring compliance with FedRAMP and ITAR (International Traffic in Arms Regulations).

4. GDPR (General Data Protection Regulation):

- **Data Processing Addendum (DPA):** AWS offers a GDPR-compliant Data Processing Addendum that details the responsibilities of AWS and its customers with respect to GDPR compliance.

- **Data Protection Features:** AWS provides services and features like AWS Identity and Access Management (IAM) and Amazon S3 bucket policies to help you comply with GDPR requirements for data protection and access control.

- **Data Location Control:** AWS allows you to choose the AWS region where your data is stored, giving you control over the geographical location of your data in compliance with GDPR.

Achieving Compliance with AWS:

Achieving compliance with various frameworks involves a shared responsibility model between AWS and the customer. While AWS manages the security of the cloud infrastructure, customers are responsible for securing their data and applications in the cloud.

To achieve compliance with a specific framework:

1. **Review AWS Documentation:** AWS provides detailed

documentation and resources for each compliance framework, outlining the shared responsibilities and best practices.

2. **Leverage AWS Services:** AWS offers a wide range of services and features that can help you achieve compliance. Familiarize yourself with these services and use them appropriately.

3. **Implement Security Controls:** Configure security controls, such as encryption, access control, and monitoring, to align with the compliance requirements of your chosen framework.

4. **Regular Auditing and Monitoring:** Implement continuous monitoring and auditing of your AWS environment to ensure ongoing compliance and address any issues promptly.

5. **Documentation and Reporting:** Maintain records of your security and compliance efforts, and be prepared to provide documentation and reports as needed for audits and assessments.

AWS provides compliance resources and artifacts, including compliance reports and certifications, to assist customers in their compliance efforts. By understanding the requirements of your target compliance framework and using AWS services effectively, you can build secure and compliant solutions on the AWS cloud platform.

Chapter 8: AWS Monitoring and Management Tools

Section 8.1: Amazon CloudWatch

Amazon CloudWatch is a monitoring and observability service provided by AWS that helps you collect and analyze data from various AWS resources and applications in real-time. CloudWatch allows you to gain insights into the operational health, performance, and resource utilization of your AWS environment. In this section, we will explore the key features and capabilities of Amazon CloudWatch.

Key Concepts:

1. Metrics:

- **Definition:** Metrics are the fundamental data points that CloudWatch collects. They represent a time-ordered set of data points and are categorized by namespaces. Metrics can include information on CPU utilization, network traffic, or custom application-specific data.

- **Example:** You can monitor the CPU utilization of an Amazon EC2 instance using the "AWS/EC2" namespace and the "CPUUtilization" metric.

2. Alarms:

- **Definition:** Alarms allow you to set thresholds on CloudWatch metrics. When a metric crosses a specified threshold for a specified duration, CloudWatch can trigger actions such as sending notifications or automatically scaling AWS resources.

- **Example:** You can create an alarm that notifies you when the CPU utilization of an EC2 instance exceeds 80% for five consecutive minutes.

3. Dashboards:

- **Definition:** Dashboards are customizable web pages that allow you to visualize CloudWatch metrics and alarms for your AWS resources in a single view. You can create and share dashboards to monitor the health of your applications.

- **Example:** You can create a dashboard that displays key performance metrics for your web application, including request latency and error rates.

4. Logs:

- **Definition:** CloudWatch Logs enables you to collect and store log data from your applications, services, and resources. You can analyze and search log data to troubleshoot issues and gain insights into your applications.

- **Example:** You can configure your application to send log data to CloudWatch Logs, making it easier to troubleshoot errors and monitor application behavior.

5. Events:

- **Definition:** CloudWatch Events allows you to respond to changes in your AWS resources by creating rules that trigger automated actions. You can use CloudWatch Events to automate tasks and react to resource events.

- **Example:** You can create an event rule that triggers an AWS Lambda function when an EC2 instance state changes to "stopped."

How CloudWatch Works:

Amazon CloudWatch collects data from various sources, including AWS services, custom applications, and on-premises resources, and makes that data available through metrics and logs. Here's how it works:

1. **Data Sources:** CloudWatch collects data from AWS resources such as EC2 instances, RDS databases, and Lambda functions. You can also send custom metrics and logs from your applications.
2. **Data Storage:** The collected data is stored securely in CloudWatch, and you can retain data for as long as needed.
3. **Metrics and Alarms:** CloudWatch provides real-time metrics that you can use to monitor the health of your resources. You can create alarms based on these metrics to notify you of potential issues.
4. **Dashboards:** You can create custom dashboards to visualize metrics and alarms from multiple sources in one place.
5. **Logs and Insights:** CloudWatch Logs allows you to store and analyze log data, enabling you to troubleshoot and

debug applications.

6. **Event Rules:** You can create event rules to automate actions in response to changes in your resources or application behavior.

CloudWatch Use Cases:

1. Resource Monitoring:

• CloudWatch helps you monitor the performance and resource utilization of your AWS resources. For example, you can monitor the CPU, memory, and disk usage of EC2 instances.

2. Application Performance:

• You can use CloudWatch to monitor application-specific metrics and set alarms to detect issues like high error rates or slow response times.

3. Scaling and Automation:

• CloudWatch alarms can trigger automated scaling actions, allowing you to scale resources up or down based on demand.

4. Log Analysis:

• CloudWatch Logs enables you to collect and analyze log data to troubleshoot issues and gain insights into application behavior.

5. Security and Compliance:

- You can use CloudWatch Events to automate security and compliance tasks by responding to events like unauthorized access attempts.

Getting Started with CloudWatch:

To get started with Amazon CloudWatch, you can follow these steps:

1. **Enable CloudWatch:** Ensure that CloudWatch is enabled for the AWS resources you want to monitor.
2. **Create Metrics and Alarms:** Define the metrics you want to monitor and set up alarms to receive notifications when specific thresholds are breached.
3. **Explore Logs:** If needed, configure CloudWatch Logs to collect log data from your applications and resources.
4. **Build Dashboards:** Create custom dashboards to visualize metrics and alarms for your resources.
5. **Automate Tasks:** Use CloudWatch Events to create event rules that automate tasks based on resource events.

Amazon CloudWatch is a powerful service that helps you gain insights into your AWS environment's operational health and performance. By effectively using CloudWatch metrics, alarms, logs, and events, you can proactively monitor and manage your AWS resources to ensure they operate efficiently and reliably.

Section 8.2: AWS CloudTrail

AWS CloudTrail is a service that provides detailed logs of the API calls made on your AWS account. These logs help you monitor and track changes and activities across your AWS infrastructure, enhancing security, compliance, and troubleshooting capabilities. In this section, we'll explore the key features and use cases of AWS CloudTrail.

Key Concepts:

1. CloudTrail Event:

• A CloudTrail event represents an API call made on your AWS resources. Each event includes information such as the user who made the call, the resource affected, the action performed, and the timestamp of the call.

2. Trails:

• A trail is a configuration that enables CloudTrail logging for a specific AWS account or organization. You can create multiple trails to capture different types of events or send logs to different destinations.

3. Log Files:

• CloudTrail log files contain recorded events and are stored in an Amazon S3 bucket of your choice. Log files are encrypted and can be analyzed to understand activities in your AWS environment.

4. Data Events:

• In addition to management events (e.g., creating an EC2 instance), CloudTrail can capture data events for supported AWS services (e.g., S3 object access). Data events provide insight into how data is accessed and modified.

5. Integrations:

- CloudTrail can be integrated with other AWS services such as Amazon CloudWatch Logs and AWS Lambda for real-time monitoring and alerting.

How CloudTrail Works:

AWS CloudTrail operates as follows:

1. **API Calls:** When an API call is made on your AWS resources (e.g., launching an EC2 instance), CloudTrail records the event, including details of the call and the AWS account that made it.
2. **Log Delivery:** CloudTrail delivers log files to an Amazon S3 bucket that you specify. Log files are encrypted to ensure data security.
3. **Event Analysis:** You can analyze log files using CloudTrail Insights or export logs to Amazon CloudWatch Logs for real-time analysis. You can also configure Amazon SNS notifications for specific events.
4. **Monitoring and Compliance:** CloudTrail logs provide visibility into who did what and when in your AWS environment. This information is valuable for security audits, compliance checks, and troubleshooting.

Use Cases for CloudTrail:

1. Security and Compliance:

• CloudTrail helps you meet security and compliance requirements by providing an audit trail of API calls. You can track changes and identify unauthorized or suspicious activities.

2. Incident Response:

• In the event of a security incident or breach, CloudTrail logs can be invaluable for investigating what happened, when it occurred, and who was involved.

3. Operational Insights:

• CloudTrail enables you to gain operational insights into your AWS environment. You can identify usage patterns, resource changes, and areas for optimization.

4. Data Access Monitoring:

• For AWS services that support data events (e.g., S3 and Lambda), CloudTrail helps you monitor and audit access to sensitive data.

5. Troubleshooting:

• When issues arise, CloudTrail logs can assist in troubleshooting by providing a history of events leading up to the problem.

Getting Started with CloudTrail:

To get started with AWS CloudTrail:

1. **Create a Trail:** Create a CloudTrail trail and specify the settings, including the S3 bucket for log storage, whether to log data events, and which AWS regions to monitor.
2. **Enable Global Services:** Decide whether to include AWS global services in your trail, such as IAM and AWS CloudFormation, which may operate across multiple regions.
3. **Configure CloudWatch Logs:** Optionally, configure CloudTrail to send logs to Amazon CloudWatch Logs for real-time analysis and alerting.
4. **Access and Analyze Logs:** After the trail is active, access and analyze CloudTrail logs using the AWS Management Console, CloudTrail Insights, or export to other tools for further analysis.
5. **Set Up Alarms:** Create CloudWatch Alarms to monitor specific events or patterns in CloudTrail logs and receive notifications when thresholds are breached.

AWS CloudTrail is a fundamental tool for enhancing the security and visibility of your AWS environment. By monitoring API calls and tracking changes, you can strengthen security, achieve compliance, and gain valuable insights into your AWS infrastructure.

Section 8.3: AWS Config

AWS Config is a powerful service that provides a detailed inventory of your AWS resources and records configuration changes over time. It helps you assess, audit, and evaluate your AWS environment's compliance with your organization's policies and best practices. In this section, we'll explore the key features and benefits of AWS Config.

Key Concepts:

1. Resource Inventory:

- AWS Config maintains an inventory of your AWS resources, including details such as resource type, location, and configuration.

2. Configuration History:

- AWS Config records changes to your resource configurations, creating a history of configuration changes over time.

3. Configuration Items:

- Configuration items are snapshots of your resources' configurations at specific points in time. You can use them to track changes and view resource details.

4. Rules and Compliance:

- AWS Config allows you to define rules based on AWS best practices or custom requirements. It evaluates your resources against these rules and reports on compliance status.

5. Config Snapshots:

- You can create snapshots of your AWS Config configurations to capture a point-in-time view of your resource states and configurations.

6. Notification and Remediation:

- AWS Config can send notifications when resources are not compliant with your rules. You can also use AWS Lambda functions for automated remediation.

How AWS Config Works:

AWS Config operates as follows:

1. **Resource Discovery:** AWS Config continuously discovers and records resource details and configurations in your AWS environment.
2. **Configuration Changes:** Whenever a resource's configuration changes (e.g., a security group rule is modified), AWS Config records the change and stores the updated configuration.
3. **Rule Evaluation:** AWS Config evaluates resources against predefined or custom rules to check for compliance. It can also identify resources that are non-compliant.
4. **History and Snapshots:** You can view the history of configuration changes and create snapshots of resource configurations for auditing purposes.
5. **Notifications and Remediation:** AWS Config can send notifications when a resource becomes non-compliant. You can configure automated remediation using AWS Lambda.

Benefits of AWS Config:

1. Resource Visibility:

• AWS Config provides a comprehensive view of your AWS resources and their configurations, making it easier to manage and troubleshoot your environment.

2. Compliance Monitoring:

• You can define rules to enforce compliance with your organization's policies and regulatory requirements, and AWS Config will continuously assess resource compliance.

3. Change Tracking:

• AWS Config keeps track of all configuration changes, helping you understand who made changes, what was changed, and when it happened.

4. Security and Governance:

• AWS Config enhances security by allowing you to monitor for security-related changes and ensures that resources adhere to security best practices.

5. Resource Relationships:

• You can visualize resource relationships and dependencies, aiding in troubleshooting and resource planning.

Getting Started with AWS Config:

To get started with AWS Config:

1. **Enable AWS Config:** In the AWS Management Console, enable AWS Config for your AWS account.
2. **Configure Recording:** Specify the AWS resources and resource types you want AWS Config to record and track.
3. **Create Rules:** Define custom rules or use predefined AWS managed rules to evaluate resource compliance.
4. **Review Configuration Changes:** Use the AWS Config dashboard to review configuration changes, resource compliance, and resource relationships.
5. **Set Up Notifications:** Configure SNS topics to receive notifications when non-compliance is detected.
6. **Remediate Non-Compliance:** Implement automated remediation using AWS Lambda functions if needed.

AWS Config is a valuable tool for maintaining control, visibility, and compliance in your AWS environment. By recording resource configurations and evaluating compliance against rules, you can ensure that your AWS resources meet security, governance, and operational requirements.

Section 8.4: AWS Systems Manager

AWS Systems Manager, often referred to as SSM, is a comprehensive service that simplifies resource and application management on AWS. It provides a unified interface to manage AWS resources and automates tasks across your infrastructure. In this section, we'll explore the key features and use cases of AWS Systems Manager.

Key Concepts:

1. Managed Instances:

- Managed instances are EC2 instances or on-premises servers that have the Systems Manager agent installed. SSM enables you to manage and configure these instances.

2. Automation Documents:

- Automation documents are predefined or custom scripts and workflows that can be executed on managed instances. They help automate common operational tasks.

3. Run Command:

- The Run Command feature allows you to execute commands remotely on multiple instances simultaneously. It's useful for tasks like software patching and configuration updates.

4. Session Manager:

- Session Manager provides secure, browser-based remote shell access to managed instances. It eliminates the need for SSH or RDP access and provides a centralized audit trail.

5. Parameter Store:

- AWS Systems Manager Parameter Store is a secure repository for storing configuration data and secrets. It's commonly used for managing application configuration.

6. Maintenance Windows:

- Maintenance Windows are scheduled timeframes during which you can perform maintenance tasks on managed instances. This helps ensure minimal disruption to operations.

How AWS Systems Manager Works:

AWS Systems Manager operates as follows:

1. **Agent Installation:** You install the Systems Manager agent on your EC2 instances or on-premises servers.
2. **Resource Discovery:** SSM continuously discovers and tracks your managed instances, collecting information about each instance's configuration.
3. **Document Execution:** You can create automation documents or use predefined ones to perform tasks on managed instances. These documents are executed remotely using SSM.
4. **Parameter Storage:** Parameter Store allows you to store and retrieve configuration data, secrets, and secure parameters centrally.
5. **Session Access:** Session Manager provides secure, auditable remote access to instances via a browser-based shell interface.
6. **Patch Management:** You can use SSM to automate

patching of operating systems and applications on managed instances.

Use Cases for AWS Systems Manager:

1. Patch Management:

• AWS Systems Manager simplifies and automates the process of patching operating systems and software on your instances.

2. Configuration Management:

• You can use Systems Manager to enforce and maintain consistent configurations across your infrastructure.

3. Application Deployment:

• Automate application deployments by creating custom automation documents and scripts.

4. Remote Access:

• Session Manager provides secure remote access to instances for troubleshooting and management.

5. Parameter Storage:

• Use Parameter Store to store and manage configuration data, secrets, and credentials.

6. Compliance and Auditing:

- AWS Systems Manager helps you maintain compliance with security and operational standards by tracking changes and configurations.

Getting Started with AWS Systems Manager:

To get started with AWS Systems Manager:

1. **Install Agent:** Install the Systems Manager agent on your managed instances.
2. **Configure IAM Roles:** Ensure that IAM roles and policies are correctly configured to grant SSM permissions.
3. **Create Automation Documents:** Define automation documents or use predefined ones for common tasks.
4. **Execute Commands:** Use Run Command to execute commands on managed instances or use Session Manager for interactive sessions.
5. **Manage Configuration:** Store and retrieve configuration data and secrets using Parameter Store.
6. **Automate Patching:** Set up patch baselines and use Systems Manager to automate patching tasks.

AWS Systems Manager is a versatile and essential service for managing and automating tasks across your AWS infrastructure. By centralizing management and providing tools for configuration, patching, and auditing, it simplifies operational tasks and enhances control over your resources.

Section 8.5: Managing and Monitoring Resources

In this section, we will explore various approaches and tools for managing and monitoring AWS resources effectively. Managing and monitoring resources is crucial for ensuring the health, performance, and security of your AWS environment.

Key Concepts:

1. AWS Management Console:

- The AWS Management Console is a web-based interface that allows you to interact with and manage your AWS resources. It provides a user-friendly graphical interface for various AWS services.

2. AWS CLI (Command Line Interface):

- The AWS CLI is a command-line tool that provides direct access to AWS services. It is particularly useful for scripting, automation, and advanced configurations.

3. AWS SDKs (Software Development Kits):

- AWS provides SDKs for various programming languages, allowing developers to interact with AWS services programmatically. SDKs simplify resource management through code.

4. AWS CloudFormation:

- AWS CloudFormation is an infrastructure-as-code (IaC) service that allows you to define and provision AWS resources using templates. It enables version-controlled resource management.

5. AWS Elastic Beanstalk:

- AWS Elastic Beanstalk is a Platform as a Service (PaaS) offering that simplifies the deployment and management of applications. It abstracts infrastructure management tasks.

6. AWS Trusted Advisor:

- AWS Trusted Advisor is an AWS service that provides real-time guidance on cost optimization, performance improvement, security best practices, and fault tolerance.

7. Amazon CloudWatch:

- Amazon CloudWatch is a monitoring and observability service for AWS resources and applications. It collects and presents metrics, logs, and alarms to help you understand resource behavior.

8. AWS CloudTrail:

- AWS CloudTrail records AWS API calls made on your account. It provides a detailed audit trail of actions taken on resources and helps with security and compliance monitoring.

AWS Resource Management Approaches:

1. Manual Management:

- Using the AWS Management Console or AWS CLI for resource provisioning and configuration, suitable for smaller environments or one-off tasks.

2. Infrastructure as Code (IaC):

- Leveraging AWS CloudFormation templates to define and deploy resources consistently and repeatably.

3. Platform Services:

- Using managed services like AWS Elastic Beanstalk for application deployment, abstracting infrastructure management.

AWS Resource Monitoring and Optimization:

1. Amazon CloudWatch Metrics:

- Configure CloudWatch to collect and visualize metrics on resource performance, set up alarms for automated responses.

2. CloudWatch Logs:

- Centralize log data from various resources for analysis and troubleshooting.

3. AWS Trusted Advisor:

- Regularly review Trusted Advisor recommendations for cost optimization, security, and performance improvement.

4. AWS Cost Explorer:

- Use Cost Explorer to analyze and visualize cost and usage data, helping to identify areas for cost optimization.

Best Practices:

1. Automation:

- Automate resource provisioning and configuration using IaC and AWS services like AWS Lambda.

2. Monitoring and Alerts:

- Implement proactive monitoring with CloudWatch metrics, logs, and alarms.

3. Cost Optimization:

- Continuously optimize costs through regular analysis, using tools like AWS Trusted Advisor and Cost Explorer.

4. Security and Compliance:

• Implement security best practices and monitor for compliance violations using AWS Config, CloudWatch, and AWS CloudTrail.

5. Resource Tagging:

• Use resource tagging to categorize and manage resources efficiently, especially for cost allocation.

Effective management and monitoring of AWS resources are essential for maintaining the reliability, security, and cost-efficiency of your cloud infrastructure. By combining the right management approaches and tools, along with a proactive monitoring and optimization strategy, you can ensure that your AWS environment meets your operational and business requirements.

Chapter 9: Automation and Orchestration with AWS

In this chapter, we dive into the world of automation and orchestration with AWS. Automation involves using technology to perform tasks with minimal human intervention, while orchestration is the coordination and management of multiple automated tasks to achieve a specific goal or workflow. AWS offers a set of powerful services and tools that enable you to automate and orchestrate various aspects of your cloud infrastructure and applications.

Section 9.1: AWS CloudFormation

AWS CloudFormation is a service that allows you to define and provision AWS infrastructure as code. Instead of manually creating and configuring resources, you can use templates to describe the desired state of your infrastructure. CloudFormation takes care of resource provisioning, updates, and deletion, making it a fundamental tool for infrastructure automation.

Key Concepts:

1. Templates:

- CloudFormation templates are JSON or YAML files that define the AWS resources and their configurations. Templates are version-controlled and can be shared and reused.

2. Stacks:

• A stack is an instance of a CloudFormation template. It represents a collection of AWS resources that are created and managed as a single unit.

3. Resources:

• Resources are the AWS components defined in your CloudFormation template, such as EC2 instances, S3 buckets, RDS databases, and more.

4. Parameters:

• Parameters allow you to customize your template's behavior by providing input values when you create or update a stack.

5. Outputs:

• Outputs enable you to retrieve information from your stack, such as the URL of a deployed application, and make it available for other AWS services to consume.

6. Mappings and Conditions:

• You can use mappings to create conditional resource configurations based on input values and conditions.

Benefits of AWS CloudFormation:

1. **Infrastructure as Code (IaC):**

– With CloudFormation, your infrastructure is defined and managed as code, enabling version control, collaboration, and repeatability.

1. **Automation:**

– CloudFormation automates the creation, update, and deletion of resources, ensuring consistency and reducing manual error-prone tasks.

1. **Scalability:**

– Easily scale your infrastructure up or down by adjusting resource counts or configurations in your template.

1. **Resource Dependencies:**

– CloudFormation automatically handles resource dependencies, ensuring that resources are created in the correct order.

1. **Rollback and Drift Detection:**

– CloudFormation provides rollback capabilities in case of failures during stack updates and can detect configuration drift.

Basic CloudFormation Workflow:

1. **Create a Template:**

– Define your infrastructure and resource configurations in a CloudFormation template.

1. **Create or Update a Stack:**

– Use the CloudFormation service to create a new stack or update an existing one by providing the template and optional parameters.

1. **CloudFormation Executes:**

– CloudFormation orchestrates the creation and configuration of resources according to the template.

1. **Stack Management:**

– Monitor and manage your stacks through the AWS Management Console, CLI, or SDKs.

Example CloudFormation Template (YAML):

Here's a simple example of a CloudFormation template that creates an EC2 instance:

```
Resources:
MyEC2Instance:
Type: AWS::EC2::Instance
Properties:
InstanceType: t2.micro
ImageId: ami-0c55b159cbfafe1f0
```

In this template, we define an EC2 instance with specific properties, such as its instance type and the Amazon Machine Image (AMI) to use.

AWS CloudFormation is a powerful tool for automating the provisioning and management of AWS resources. It allows you to define your infrastructure in a declarative manner and ensures that your environment remains consistent and easily reproducible. In the following sections, we'll explore more AWS automation and orchestration services and tools that complement CloudFormation.

Section 9.2: AWS Elastic Beanstalk

AWS Elastic Beanstalk is a Platform as a Service (PaaS) offering that simplifies the deployment and management of applications. It abstracts the underlying infrastructure, allowing developers to focus on building and deploying their applications without worrying about server provisioning and configuration.

Key Concepts:

1. Application Environments:

- In Elastic Beanstalk, you create environments for your applications. An environment is a collection of AWS resources, including Amazon EC2 instances, that host your application.

2. Application Versions:

- You deploy your application to Elastic Beanstalk as versions. Each version represents a snapshot of your application's code and configurations.

3. Supported Platforms:

- Elastic Beanstalk supports multiple programming languages and platforms, including Java, .NET, PHP, Node.js, Python, Ruby, Go, and Docker.

4. Environment Configurations:

- You can customize the environment configurations, including instance types, scaling settings, and database connections, to meet your application's requirements.

5. Managed Updates:

- Elastic Beanstalk provides managed platform updates, including operating system and runtime updates, to ensure that your environment stays secure and up-to-date.

6. Monitoring and Logging:

- Elastic Beanstalk integrates with Amazon CloudWatch for monitoring and provides logs for troubleshooting and performance analysis.

7. Auto Scaling:

- You can configure auto-scaling for your Elastic Beanstalk environments to automatically adjust the number of instances based on traffic.

Elastic Beanstalk Workflow:

1. Create an Application:

– Start by creating an Elastic Beanstalk application, which serves as a container for your environments.

1. Create an Environment:

– Within your application, create one or more environments with specific configurations and settings.

1. Deploy Application Version:

– Upload your application code as a version and deploy it to the desired environment.

1. Elastic Beanstalk Manages Resources:

– Elastic Beanstalk automatically provisions and manages the necessary AWS resources, including EC2 instances, load balancers, and databases.

1. Monitor and Scale:

– Monitor your environment's performance and configure auto-scaling rules if needed.

1. Update Application:

– When you make changes to your application, create a new version, and update your environment.

Example Elastic Beanstalk Configuration (YAML):

Here's an example configuration file (ebextensions/myapp.config) that specifies environment settings for an Elastic Beanstalk environment:

```
option_settings:
- namespace: aws:autoscaling:launchconfiguration
option_name: InstanceType
value: t2.micro
- namespace: aws:elasticbeanstalk:container:python
```

option_name: WSGIPath
value: application.py
- namespace: aws:elasticbeanstalk:environment
option_name: EnvironmentType
value: SingleInstance

In this configuration, we define instance type, the WSGI path for a Python application, and the environment type.

Elastic Beanstalk simplifies the deployment and management of web applications, making it an ideal choice for developers who want to focus on their code rather than infrastructure management. It provides scalability, reliability, and easy integration with other AWS services, making it suitable for a wide range of application types and workloads. In the following sections, we'll explore more AWS automation and orchestration services and tools that complement Elastic Beanstalk.

Section 9.3: AWS Step Functions

AWS Step Functions is a serverless orchestration service that allows you to coordinate multiple AWS services into serverless workflows. It provides a visual way to design, run, and monitor workflows, making it easy to build applications with complex, multi-step logic.

Key Concepts:

1. State Machines:

- In AWS Step Functions, workflows are defined as state machines. Each state machine is a collection of states and transitions that define the workflow's logic.

2. *States:*

- States represent individual steps or tasks in your workflow. AWS Step Functions offers various state types, including AWS service integrations, choice states, and more.

3. *Execution History:*

- AWS Step Functions keeps a detailed execution history of each state machine run, allowing you to troubleshoot and review the workflow's progress.

4. *Error Handling:*

- You can define error handling and retries for each state, ensuring robustness in case of failures.

5. *Input and Output Data:*

- Pass input data to your states, and collect output data from states as they execute. This enables data flow between states in the workflow.

6. *Visual Workflow Designer:*

- AWS Step Functions provides a visual designer in the AWS Management Console to create and edit state machine definitions.

Benefits of AWS Step Functions:

1. Simplified Orchestration:

– Step Functions abstracts the complexity of orchestrating multiple AWS services, making it easier to design and manage workflows.

1. Built-In Error Handling:

– Implement error handling and retries directly in your state machine definition, improving the reliability of your workflows.

1. Real-time Monitoring:

– Monitor the execution of your state machines in real-time, view detailed logs, and set up CloudWatch alarms for notifications.

1. Integration with AWS Services:

– Integrate with various AWS services, such as Lambda, ECS, SNS, SQS, and more, to build versatile workflows.

1. Scalability:

– AWS Step Functions automatically scales to handle high volumes of workflow executions.

State Machine Definition (JSON):

Here's a simplified example of a state machine definition in JSON that coordinates AWS Lambda functions:

```
{
"StartAt": "HelloWorld",
"States": {
"HelloWorld": {
"Type": "Task",
"Resource":
"arn:aws:lambda:us-east-1:123456789012:function:HelloWorldFunction
"End": true
}
}
}
```

In this example, the state machine starts at the "HelloWorld" state, which executes a Lambda function and ends the workflow.

AWS Step Functions is valuable for creating workflows that involve multiple AWS services, such as data processing pipelines, application integrations, and more. It simplifies complex orchestration tasks, improves visibility into workflow execution, and enhances the overall reliability of your applications. In the following sections, we'll explore additional AWS automation and orchestration services and tools.

Section 9.4: Serverless Application Model (SAM)

The AWS Serverless Application Model (SAM) is an open-source framework for building serverless applications on AWS. It extends AWS CloudFormation to provide a simplified way to define serverless resources and the associated AWS infrastructure as code. SAM makes it easier to develop, deploy, and manage serverless applications.

Key Concepts:

1. Serverless Resources:

• SAM introduces resource types specific to serverless applications, such as AWS Lambda functions, API Gateway APIs, and Amazon DynamoDB tables.

2. Template Syntax:

• SAM templates use a simplified syntax that reduces boilerplate code compared to traditional CloudFormation templates. This makes it easier to define serverless resources and their properties.

3. Local Development:

• SAM CLI (Command Line Interface) allows developers to test and debug serverless applications locally before deploying them to AWS.

4. Lambda Layers:

• SAM supports Lambda Layers, allowing you to share code and libraries across multiple Lambda functions.

5. Event Sources:

• Define event sources, such as API Gateway endpoints, S3 buckets, and DynamoDB streams, directly in your SAM template.

6. Integrated Deployment:

- Use SAM CLI or AWS CloudFormation to deploy your serverless application. SAM automatically packages and deploys your application code and resources.

SAM Template Example:

Here's a simplified SAM template example that defines a serverless application with an API Gateway endpoint and a Lambda function:

```
AWSTemplateFormatVersion: '2010-09-09'
Transform: 'AWS::Serverless-2016-10-31'
Description: My Serverless Application
Resources:
MyApi:
Type: 'AWS::Serverless::Api'
Properties:
StageName: Prod
MyFunction:
Type: 'AWS::Serverless::Function'
Properties:
CodeUri: ./src/
Handler: app.lambda_handler
Runtime: python3.8
Events:
HelloWorld:
Type: Api
Properties:
Path: /hello
Method: get
```

In this example, the template defines an API Gateway with a "/hello" endpoint that triggers a Lambda function. SAM's simplified syntax makes it easy to understand the application's structure.

SAM CLI:

To develop and test your serverless application locally, you can use the SAM CLI. It provides commands for running and debugging Lambda functions, generating sample payloads, and packaging and deploying your application.

SAM simplifies the development and deployment of serverless applications on AWS, making it an excellent choice for building scalable and cost-effective serverless solutions. It abstracts many of the complexities associated with serverless application development, allowing developers to focus on their code and business logic. In the next section, we'll explore building DevOps pipelines for continuous integration and continuous deployment (CI/CD) of serverless applications.

Section 9.5: Building DevOps Pipelines

DevOps practices are essential for automating and streamlining the development, deployment, and management of applications in AWS. Building DevOps pipelines for serverless applications helps ensure a consistent and efficient development and release process.

Key Components of a Serverless DevOps Pipeline:

1. Source Control:

- Use a source code repository (e.g., Git) to manage your serverless application code. This provides version control and collaboration capabilities.

2. Continuous Integration (CI):

- Set up CI pipelines to automatically build, test, and package your serverless application whenever changes are pushed to the source code repository.

3. Artifact Repository:

- Store the packaged artifacts, such as AWS SAM templates and Lambda deployment packages, in an artifact repository for versioning and easy access during deployments.

4. Deployment Automation:

- Use automation tools like AWS CodeDeploy, AWS CloudFormation, or AWS SAM to deploy your serverless application to multiple environments (e.g., development, staging, production).

5. Testing and Validation:

- Implement automated testing, including unit tests and integration tests, to validate the functionality and performance of your serverless application.

6. Infrastructure as Code (IaC):

- Define your AWS infrastructure, including serverless resources, using infrastructure as code (IaC) principles. Tools like AWS CloudFormation or AWS CDK can help with this.

7. Continuous Deployment (CD):

• Automate the deployment of your serverless application to different environments, ensuring consistency and reducing manual intervention.

8. Monitoring and Logging:

• Set up monitoring and logging for your serverless application using AWS services like Amazon CloudWatch. Monitor application performance and respond to issues proactively.

Sample DevOps Pipeline Configuration:

Here's an example of a simplified serverless DevOps pipeline using AWS services:

1. **Source Control**: Developers push code changes to a Git repository (e.g., GitHub).
2. **Continuous Integration (CI)**: A CI/CD tool (e.g., AWS CodePipeline) detects changes in the repository and triggers the CI process.
3. **Build and Package**: During the CI process, the serverless application is built, tested, and packaged into deployment artifacts. AWS SAM or custom scripts can assist with this.
4. **Artifact Repository**: The packaged artifacts are stored in an artifact repository like Amazon S3 or AWS CodeArtifact.
5. **Deployment Automation**: AWS CodePipeline triggers a deployment process using AWS CloudFormation or AWS SAM to create/update serverless resources.
6. **Testing and Validation**: Automated tests, including unit

tests and integration tests, are executed to validate the application's functionality.

7. **Infrastructure as Code (IaC)**: The serverless infrastructure is defined using AWS CloudFormation templates or AWS CDK scripts.
8. **Continuous Deployment (CD)**: The application is deployed to the desired environment (e.g., development, staging, production) with minimal manual intervention.
9. **Monitoring and Logging**: Monitoring and logging configurations are automatically applied, allowing for real-time visibility into the application's behavior.

By implementing such a DevOps pipeline for your serverless applications, you can achieve faster development cycles, improved code quality, and better collaboration among development, testing, and operations teams. Automated testing and deployment processes also enhance the reliability and stability of your serverless applications.

Chapter 10: High Availability and Scalability

Section 10.1: AWS Auto Scaling

High availability and scalability are crucial considerations when deploying applications in the cloud. AWS offers various services and features to help achieve these goals, and one key service is AWS Auto Scaling.

Understanding AWS Auto Scaling:

AWS Auto Scaling is a service that automatically adjusts the number and capacity of your Amazon EC2 instances or other resources to maintain application availability and performance at the desired levels. It helps you manage the load on your applications by dynamically scaling resources in and out based on conditions you define.

Key Concepts:

1. Auto Scaling Groups (ASGs):

  • An Auto Scaling group is a logical grouping of Amazon EC2 instances that are managed together. ASGs are the core building blocks for automatic scaling in AWS.

2. Scaling Policies:

  • Scaling policies define the conditions and actions for scaling in or out. You can create scaling policies to adjust capacity based on metrics like CPU utilization, network traffic, or custom CloudWatch metrics.

3. Scaling Triggers:

• Scaling triggers are events that initiate the scaling process. They can be based on CloudWatch alarms, scheduled actions, or demand-driven triggers.

4. Instance Launch Configuration:

• An instance launch configuration defines the configuration settings for the instances in an ASG. It specifies the Amazon Machine Image (AMI), instance type, security groups, and more.

5. Scaling Plans:

• Scaling plans help you optimize your ASGs for cost, performance, and availability. They provide recommendations for adjusting capacity to match your application's needs.

How AWS Auto Scaling Works:

1. Monitoring Metrics:

– AWS Auto Scaling monitors the specified metrics using Amazon CloudWatch. These metrics can include CPU utilization, network traffic, or custom application-specific metrics.

1. Scaling Policies:

– You define scaling policies that specify how to react to changes in monitored metrics. For example, you can create a scaling policy that adds instances when CPU utilization exceeds a certain threshold.

1. **Scaling Actions:**

– When a scaling policy's conditions are met, AWS Auto Scaling takes action. It can add or remove instances from the Auto Scaling group to maintain the desired metric levels.

1. **Adjusting Capacity:**

– Instances are automatically launched or terminated based on the defined scaling actions. This ensures that your application scales seamlessly in response to changing traffic or resource demands.

Benefits of AWS Auto Scaling:

• **High Availability:** AWS Auto Scaling helps ensure that your application can handle traffic spikes and maintain availability even if instances fail.

• **Cost Optimization:** You can optimize costs by scaling in during periods of low demand and scaling out during peak traffic, reducing the number of idle instances.

• **Improved Performance:** Auto Scaling helps maintain consistent application performance by automatically adjusting capacity to meet performance targets.

- **Elasticity:** Your application can scale up or down quickly in response to changes in demand, ensuring a responsive user experience.

In the next sections, we'll explore other high availability and scalability features and services on AWS, including Amazon Elastic Load Balancing, Multi-AZ deployments, content delivery, and best practices for designing resilient architectures.

Section 10.2: Amazon Elastic Load Balancing

Amazon Elastic Load Balancing (ELB) is a highly scalable and fully managed load balancing service provided by AWS. It plays a crucial role in achieving high availability and scalability for your applications by distributing incoming traffic across multiple Amazon EC2 instances or other resources. ELB offers several benefits and features that enhance the performance and fault tolerance of your applications.

Key Features of Amazon Elastic Load Balancing:

1. Automatic Traffic Distribution:

- ELB automatically distributes incoming application traffic across multiple targets, such as EC2 instances, containers, or IP addresses. This helps evenly distribute the load and ensures that no single resource is overwhelmed.

2. High Availability:

- ELB is designed for high availability. It automatically detects unhealthy instances and redirects traffic to healthy instances, ensuring that your application remains available even if individual resources fail.

3. Managed Service:

• ELB is a fully managed service, which means AWS takes care of all the operational aspects, such as hardware provisioning, patching, and scaling, so you can focus on your application.

4. Load Balancer Types:

• ELB offers three types of load balancers:

– **Application Load Balancer (ALB):** Best suited for routing HTTP/HTTPS traffic and providing advanced features like content-based routing and path-based routing.

– **Network Load Balancer (NLB):** Ideal for handling TCP/UDP traffic and offers high performance with low-latency routing.

– **Classic Load Balancer (CLB):** The original load balancer type, suitable for both HTTP/HTTPS and TCP/UDP traffic.

5. Integrated with AWS Services:

• ELB integrates seamlessly with other AWS services such as Amazon EC2, Auto Scaling, and AWS Certificate Manager, making it easy to set up secure and highly available applications.

How Amazon Elastic Load Balancing Works:

1. **Client Requests:**

– When a client sends a request to your application, it resolves the DNS name associated with the ELB. ELB then routes the request to one of the healthy targets.

1. **Distribution Algorithm:**

– ELB uses a distribution algorithm, which can be round-robin or least connections, to determine which target should receive the request. This ensures that the load is distributed fairly.

1. **Health Checks:**

– ELB regularly performs health checks on registered targets to identify unhealthy instances. Unhealthy instances are removed from the load balancer's rotation.

1. **Fault Tolerance:**

– ELB is designed for fault tolerance. If an ELB node fails, traffic is automatically redirected to healthy nodes, ensuring minimal disruption.

Use Cases for Amazon Elastic Load Balancing:

• **Web Applications:** ELB is commonly used to distribute traffic across web servers in a scalable and fault-tolerant manner.

- **Microservices:** In a microservices architecture, ELB can route requests to different microservices based on URL paths, making it ideal for containerized applications.

- **Multi-Region Deployments:** ELB can be used to distribute traffic across multiple regions to improve global application availability.

- **SSL Termination:** ELB can terminate SSL/TLS encryption, offloading the decryption process from backend instances and improving performance.

- **IPv6 Support:** ELB provides IPv6 support, enabling applications to serve clients over IPv6 networks.

In the next section, we'll explore the concept of Multi-AZ (Availability Zone) deployments, which further enhance the availability and fault tolerance of your applications on AWS.

Section 10.3: Multi-AZ Deployments

In Amazon Web Services (AWS), Availability Zones (AZs) are data centers located in different geographic regions within a specific AWS Region. Multi-AZ deployments are a crucial strategy for ensuring high availability and fault tolerance for your applications. By distributing your resources across multiple AZs, you can protect your application from failures in a single AZ and provide a more reliable experience to your users.

Key Concepts:

1. Availability Zones (AZs):

- An AWS Region typically consists of multiple Availability Zones. These AZs are isolated from each other and connected through high-speed, low-latency links.

2. Multi-AZ Deployment:

- A Multi-AZ deployment involves replicating your application resources in multiple AZs. For example, you might have an Amazon EC2 instance running your web application in one AZ and a replica of that instance in another AZ.

3. High Availability (HA):

- Multi-AZ deployments are a key component of achieving high availability. If one AZ experiences an issue, traffic is automatically routed to healthy resources in another AZ.

4. Load Balancing:

- Load balancers, such as Amazon Elastic Load Balancing (ELB), play a crucial role in distributing traffic evenly across resources in different AZs. This ensures that no single AZ becomes a bottleneck.

Benefits of Multi-AZ Deployments:

1. Fault Tolerance:

– Multi-AZ deployments protect your application from AZ-level failures. If an AZ becomes unavailable due to a hardware failure or other issue, your application can continue running in another AZ without interruption.

1. Improved Reliability:

– By distributing your resources, you reduce the risk of single points of failure. This enhances the overall reliability of your application.

1. Automatic Failover:

– AWS services like Amazon RDS (Relational Database Service) and Amazon Elasticache can be set up for Multi-AZ deployments with automatic failover. In the event of a primary resource failure, traffic is redirected to a standby resource.

1. Disaster Recovery:

– Multi-AZ deployments also serve as a foundation for disaster recovery strategies. You can replicate your resources to a different AWS Region for even greater resilience.

Implementing Multi-AZ Deployments:

Here's a high-level overview of how to implement a Multi-AZ deployment:

1.   **Identify Critical Resources:**

– Determine which AWS resources are critical for your application's availability, such as databases, web servers, or application servers.

1.   **Utilize AWS Services:**

– AWS provides services like Amazon RDS, Amazon Elasticache, and Amazon S3 that offer Multi-AZ support. Utilize these services to create redundant, Multi-AZ architectures.

1.   **Configure Load Balancing:**

– Use load balancers, such as Amazon Elastic Load Balancing, to distribute incoming traffic across resources in different AZs. This ensures a balanced workload and fault tolerance.

1.   **Regular Testing:**

– Periodically test your Multi-AZ setup by intentionally simulating failures. Ensure that failover mechanisms work as expected.

By implementing Multi-AZ deployments, you can enhance the availability and reliability of your AWS-hosted applications, providing a seamless experience for your users even in the face of unexpected events. In the next section, we'll explore the concept of content delivery and caching for optimizing the performance of your applications.

Section 10.4: Content Delivery and Caching

Content delivery and caching are essential strategies for optimizing the performance of your web applications and reducing latency for end-users. Amazon Web Services (AWS) offers various services and tools to help you implement effective content delivery and caching solutions.

Key Concepts:

1. Content Delivery Network (CDN):

- A CDN is a distributed network of servers that cache and deliver content, such as images, videos, and web pages, from locations closer to the end-users. This reduces the latency and load on your origin server.

2. Amazon CloudFront:

- Amazon CloudFront is AWS's CDN service. It distributes content through a global network of edge locations. It integrates seamlessly with other AWS services and supports various content types.

3. Caching:

- Caching involves storing frequently accessed data in a temporary storage location (cache) for faster retrieval. AWS offers caching solutions like Amazon ElastiCache for Redis and Memcached.

4. Cache Hit and Miss:

- A cache hit occurs when requested data is found in the cache, resulting in faster response times. A cache miss occurs when the data is not in the cache, requiring retrieval from the origin server.

Benefits of Content Delivery and Caching:

1. Reduced Latency:

– CDNs deliver content from edge locations geographically closer to users, reducing the time it takes to fetch content.

1. Improved Scalability:

– Caching offloads traffic from your origin server, allowing it to handle more concurrent requests and scale efficiently.

1. Cost Savings:

– By reducing the load on your origin server, content delivery and caching can help lower your operational costs.

1. Better User Experience:

– Faster page load times and responsive applications lead to a better user experience and higher user satisfaction.

Implementing Content Delivery and Caching:

To leverage content delivery and caching effectively:

1. **Choose the Right CDN:**

– Evaluate your requirements and choose a CDN service that suits your needs. Amazon CloudFront is a popular choice due to its integration with AWS services and global reach.

1. **Cache Static Content:**

– Cache static assets like images, CSS, and JavaScript files at the edge locations to reduce the load on your origin server.

1. **Set Cache Policies:**

– Configure caching rules and policies to control how content is cached and for how long. This ensures that frequently accessed content remains in the cache.

1. **Dynamic Content Caching:**

– For dynamic content, consider using caching solutions like Amazon ElastiCache for Redis or Memcached. These can help reduce database load and improve response times.

1. **Cache Invalidation:**

– Implement cache invalidation strategies to ensure that updated content is reflected in the cache. This prevents users from seeing stale data.

1. **Monitoring and Optimization:**

– Regularly monitor CDN and cache performance. Adjust cache policies and configurations based on usage patterns and traffic.

Here's a simple example of using Amazon CloudFront for content delivery:

1. Create an Amazon S3 bucket to store your static content (e.g., images, CSS files).

2. Configure an Amazon CloudFront distribution with your S3 bucket as the origin.

3. Set caching behavior and TTL (Time to Live) settings to control how content is cached.

4. Update your web application to reference the CloudFront URL for static assets.

By implementing content delivery and caching strategies, you can significantly enhance the performance and reliability of your web applications, providing a better experience for your users while reducing operational costs. In the next section, we'll explore best practices for designing resilient and fault-tolerant architectures.

Section 10.5: Designing for Resilience

Designing for resilience in your AWS architecture is critical to ensure that your applications can continue to operate reliably even in the face of failures or unexpected events. Resilience involves building systems that can adapt to disruptions and maintain essential functionality. AWS provides several services and best practices to help you design resilient architectures.

Key Concepts:

1. Availability Zones (AZs):

- AWS divides regions into multiple availability zones (AZs), each with its own power, cooling, and networking. Distributing resources across AZs helps mitigate the impact of AZ-level failures.

2. Multi-Region Architectures:

- To achieve higher levels of resilience, you can deploy your application in multiple AWS regions. This ensures that even if an entire region experiences issues, your application can continue to operate from another region.

3. Load Balancing:

- AWS offers load balancing services like Amazon Elastic Load Balancing (ELB) to distribute traffic evenly across multiple instances or AZs. Load balancers can automatically reroute traffic away from unhealthy instances.

4. Auto Scaling:

- Auto Scaling automatically adjusts the number of instances in your application based on traffic or resource utilization. This helps maintain consistent performance during traffic spikes and reduces costs during low-demand periods.

5. Data Backup and Recovery:

• Implement regular data backup and recovery strategies, including automated backups, snapshots, and replication. AWS services like Amazon RDS and Amazon S3 offer built-in data protection features.

6. Monitoring and Alarms:

• Use AWS CloudWatch to monitor resource utilization and set up alarms to alert you when thresholds are exceeded. Proactive monitoring helps identify issues before they impact users.

Best Practices for Designing Resilient Architectures:

1. Distributed Systems:

– Design applications as distributed systems, with components running in multiple AZs or regions. Use services like Amazon S3, Amazon RDS Multi-AZ, and Amazon ElastiCache for redundancy.

1. Fault Tolerance:

– Identify potential points of failure and implement fault-tolerant design patterns, such as retry mechanisms, circuit breakers, and graceful degradation.

1. Decoupling Components:

– Use message queues (e.g., Amazon SQS) and event-driven architectures to decouple components of your application. This isolates failures and prevents cascading issues.

1. **Chaos Engineering:**

– Conduct chaos engineering experiments to proactively test how your system responds to failures. Tools like AWS Fault Injection Simulator can help simulate failures in a controlled environment.

1. **Disaster Recovery Plans:**

– Develop and test disaster recovery plans to recover from catastrophic failures. Implement cross-region replication for critical data.

1. **Documentation and Runbooks:**

– Maintain documentation and runbooks that describe how to respond to common failure scenarios. Ensure that your team is well-prepared to handle incidents.

Here's an example of using Amazon RDS Multi-AZ for database resilience:

1. Create an Amazon RDS database instance and enable Multi-AZ deployment.

2. In the event of a primary database instance failure, Amazon RDS will automatically fail over to the standby instance in another AZ.

3. Update your application's database connection settings to use the endpoint provided by Amazon RDS, which automatically routes traffic to the primary instance.

Designing for resilience is an ongoing process that involves planning, testing, and continuous improvement. By following best practices and leveraging AWS services, you can build robust and reliable architectures that can withstand failures and provide a seamless experience to your users. In the next chapter, we'll explore cost optimization strategies to manage your AWS expenses effectively.

Chapter 11: Cost Optimization on AWS

Section 11.1: AWS Cost Explorer

AWS Cost Explorer is a powerful tool that helps you analyze your AWS spending and make informed decisions to optimize your costs. It provides various features and functionalities to gain insights into your AWS usage and spending patterns.

Understanding Cost Explorer

AWS Cost Explorer allows you to:

- **Visualize Costs**: You can create visual representations of your AWS spending data, making it easier to understand and identify areas where cost optimization is needed.

- **Analyze Historical Data**: Cost Explorer provides historical cost and usage data, allowing you to track changes over time and make informed budgeting decisions.

- **Create Custom Reports**: You can create custom reports and filter data based on various parameters like service, region, tags, and more. This helps you focus on specific areas of your AWS infrastructure.

- **Forecast Future Costs**: Cost Explorer offers cost forecasting, helping you predict future expenses based on your historical data and usage patterns.

Cost Explorer Dashboards

AWS Cost Explorer offers different dashboards to view your spending data:

1. **Costs by Service**: This dashboard provides a breakdown of your spending by AWS service. You can quickly identify which services are consuming the most resources and costs.
2. **Costs by Linked Account**: If you have multiple AWS accounts linked under an organization, this dashboard lets you analyze spending for each account individually.
3. **Monthly Spend**: The monthly spend dashboard shows your monthly cost trends, helping you identify any sudden spikes or unusual spending patterns.
4. **Reservation Utilization**: If you use AWS Reserved Instances (RIs), this dashboard helps you track the utilization of your reserved capacity.

Using Cost Explorer for Cost Optimization

Here are some ways you can use AWS Cost Explorer for cost optimization:

- **Identify Underutilized Resources**: Analyze your spending data to find instances or services that are underutilized or not needed. You can then consider resizing or terminating them to save costs.

- **Spotting Anomalies**: Cost Explorer can help you spot anomalies or unexpected spending increases. Investigate these spikes to ensure they are not due to inefficiencies or errors.

- **Budget Management**: Set up budgets and alerts in AWS Cost Explorer to get notified when your spending exceeds predefined thresholds. This helps you proactively manage your costs.

- **Optimize Reserved Instances**: If you use RIs, analyze their utilization and make adjustments to your reservations to ensure you're getting the most value out of them.

- **Forecasting**: Use the cost forecasting feature to plan your future budget and understand how changes in your infrastructure might impact costs.

AWS Cost Explorer is a valuable tool for any AWS user looking to optimize their cloud spending. By leveraging its capabilities, you can make data-driven decisions to reduce costs while still meeting your performance and reliability requirements.

Section 11.2: Cost Allocation Tags

Cost allocation tags are a fundamental feature of AWS that help you categorize and allocate your resource costs. By assigning tags to your AWS resources, you can gain better visibility into how your spending is distributed across different categories or departments within your organization. This is essential for cost optimization, budgeting, and chargeback.

Understanding Cost Allocation Tags

Cost allocation tags are metadata labels that you attach to AWS resources. These tags consist of a key-value pair, where the key represents the category or attribute, and the value is the specific label or identifier. For example, you can use tags to represent departments, projects, environments (e.g., production or development), and more.

Here's why cost allocation tags are valuable:

1. **Resource Categorization**: Tags allow you to categorize your AWS resources based on your organization's needs. This helps you understand which resources belong to specific projects or departments.
2. **Cost Attribution**: Tags provide a way to attribute costs to different cost centers or teams within your organization. This is crucial for accurate cost tracking.
3. **Cost Allocation**: AWS uses tags to allocate costs in various AWS Cost Explorer reports and billing statements. You can view costs broken down by tag, making it easier to analyze spending patterns.
4. **Budgeting**: When setting up budgets in AWS, you can use tags as filters. For example, you can create a budget that tracks costs for a specific project or department based on tags.
5. **Cost Optimization**: Tags help you identify areas where cost optimization is needed. You can spot high-spending tags and take action to reduce costs for those categories.

Applying Cost Allocation Tags

To apply cost allocation tags to AWS resources, you can use the AWS Management Console, AWS CLI, AWS SDKs, or AWS CloudFormation templates. Here's a basic example of how to apply tags to an EC2 instance using the AWS CLI:

aws ec2 create-tags—resources i-1234567890abcdef0—tags Key=Department,Value=Finance Key=Project,Value=AppX

In this example, two tags are applied to an EC2 instance: one indicating the department as "Finance" and another indicating the project as "AppX."

Using Cost Allocation Tags for Cost Analysis

Once you've tagged your resources, you can leverage tags in AWS Cost Explorer and AWS Billing and Cost Management reports. Here's how you can use tags for cost analysis:

- **Custom Reports**: Create custom reports in AWS Cost Explorer and filter the data by tags. For example, you can create a report that shows the monthly costs for each department or project.

- **Cost Explorer Dashboards**: Cost Explorer offers dashboards that allow you to view spending by tags, helping you identify areas of high expenditure.

- **Budgets**: When setting up budgets, you can use tags as filters to create budgets that are specific to certain tags. This enables you to monitor and control spending for different categories.

- **Monthly Billing Statements**: Tags are also included in your monthly AWS billing statements, making it easy to see the cost allocation for each tag.

Best Practices for Cost Allocation Tags

Here are some best practices for effectively using cost allocation tags:

1. **Consistent Naming**: Maintain a consistent naming convention for your tags to ensure clarity and consistency across your organization.

2. **Automate Tagging**: Use automation scripts or AWS services like AWS Lambda to automatically apply tags to resources based on predefined rules.
3. **Regular Review**: Periodically review your tags and ensure they accurately reflect your organization's structure and resource ownership.
4. **Education**: Educate your teams about the importance of tagging and how it impacts cost allocation and optimization.

By effectively utilizing cost allocation tags, you can gain better control over your AWS spending and make informed decisions to optimize costs within your organization.

Section 11.3: EC2 Instance Types and Pricing

Amazon Elastic Compute Cloud (Amazon EC2) provides a wide range of instance types optimized for various workloads and use cases. Understanding EC2 instance types and pricing is crucial for optimizing costs while meeting your performance and resource requirements.

EC2 Instance Types

EC2 instance types are designed to cater to specific compute, memory, storage, and network requirements. They are grouped into several families, each tailored for different purposes. Some common EC2 instance families include:

1. **General Purpose (M5)**: These instances are balanced and offer a good mix of compute, memory, and network resources. They are suitable for a wide range of applications.
2. **Compute Optimized (C5)**: These instances are optimized

for CPU-intensive workloads and provide high compute power.

3. **Memory Optimized (R5)**: R5 instances are ideal for memory-intensive applications that require a large amount of RAM.

4. **Storage Optimized (I3)**: I3 instances are optimized for high-speed, low-latency storage, making them suitable for databases and data warehousing.

5. **Accelerated Computing (P3, G4)**: These instances feature powerful GPUs and are designed for machine learning, graphics-intensive tasks, and high-performance computing.

6. **Burstable Performance (T2, T3)**: T2 and T3 instances are cost-effective options with burstable CPU performance for workloads with occasional spikes in demand.

7. **High I/O (D2)**: D2 instances are designed for applications that require high disk throughput and sequential I/O.

8. **FPGA Instances (F1)**: These instances come with field-programmable gate arrays (FPGAs) and are suitable for custom hardware acceleration.

9. **Instances with Local Storage (H1, I3, D2)**: Some instances come with local NVMe SSD storage, which can be advantageous for specific workloads that require fast access to local storage.

Instance Sizes

Within each EC2 instance family, there are different instance sizes. Instances with higher numbers in their names generally offer more resources, including CPU and memory. For example, an m5.large instance provides more resources than an m5.small instance.

Pricing Models

EC2 instances can be billed using various pricing models:

1. **On-Demand**: With on-demand pricing, you pay for compute capacity by the hour or by the second (for some instance types) with no upfront costs or long-term commitments. This is suitable for short-term or variable workloads.

2. **Reserved Instances (RIs)**: RIs allow you to reserve instance capacity for a specific period (e.g., one or three years) in exchange for significant cost savings compared to on-demand pricing. RIs are suitable for stable workloads with predictable resource requirements.

3. **Spot Instances**: Spot instances allow you to bid on unused EC2 capacity, potentially providing substantial cost savings. However, they can be terminated with short notice when the capacity is needed elsewhere. Spot instances are ideal for fault-tolerant and flexible workloads.

4. **Dedicated Hosts**: Dedicated hosts provide physical servers dedicated to your use. They are suitable for compliance and licensing requirements that necessitate physical isolation.

Pricing Considerations

When selecting EC2 instances and pricing models, consider the following factors:

- **Workload Characteristics**: Understand your workload's resource requirements, such as CPU, memory, and storage. Choose instance types that match these requirements.

- **Cost Optimization**: Optimize costs by selecting the right pricing model. For predictable workloads, consider reserved instances. For flexible or fault-tolerant workloads, spot instances can be cost-effective.

- **Instance Size**: Choose the appropriate instance size to avoid underutilization or resource constraints. Monitor your workload's performance to make adjustments as needed.

- **Auto Scaling**: Implement auto scaling to dynamically adjust the number of instances based on workload demand. This helps control costs and ensures performance.

- **Monitoring and Reporting**: Utilize AWS monitoring tools like Amazon CloudWatch to gain insights into instance utilization and spending. Use cost allocation tags to track spending by project, department, or environment.

By carefully selecting EC2 instance types and pricing models based on your workload characteristics and usage patterns, you can effectively manage your AWS costs while maintaining the performance and scalability needed for your applications.

Section 11.4: Reserved Instances and Savings Plans

Amazon Web Services (AWS) offers several pricing options to help you optimize costs, including Reserved Instances (RIs) and Savings Plans. These options allow you to save significantly on your EC2 instance costs compared to on-demand pricing. In this section, we'll explore RIs and Savings Plans and how to use them effectively.

Reserved Instances (RIs)

Reserved Instances are a cost-saving option that allows you to reserve EC2 capacity for a specified duration, typically one or three years. By committing to a specific instance type in a particular region, you receive a significant discount compared to on-demand pricing. Here are key points to consider:

- **Instance Flexibility**: RIs offer instance size flexibility, allowing you to change the instance size within the same instance family, as long as it's of equal or lesser value. This flexibility is useful for adapting to changing workload requirements.

- **Availability Zone (AZ) Flexibility**: Most RIs provide regional flexibility, meaning you can use them in any Availability Zone within the chosen region. However, some RIs offer specific AZ or instance type combinations for additional savings.

- **Convertible RIs**: AWS offers convertible RIs that allow you to change the instance family or operating system, providing more flexibility for evolving workloads.

- **Payment Options**: RIs can be paid for upfront, partially upfront, or with no upfront payment, with varying discount levels based on the payment option.

- **Term Length**: RIs are available in one-year and three-year terms, with three-year terms offering higher savings.

Savings Plans

Savings Plans offer more flexibility compared to RIs. They provide a discount based on your hourly commitment rather than a specific instance type or region. Here's what you need to know about Savings Plans:

- **Commitment**: With Savings Plans, you commit to a specific amount per hour (e.g., $10 per hour) for a one- or three-year term. This commitment can be applied to any EC2 instance family or region, giving you more flexibility.

- **Instance Family and Region Flexibility**: Savings Plans offer the flexibility to switch between instance families and regions to match your changing workload needs.

- **EC2 and Fargate Usage**: Savings Plans cover not only EC2 instances but also AWS Fargate, giving you broader coverage for compute resources.

- **Automatic Application**: Savings Plans are automatically applied to your eligible usage, reducing the need to manage reservations manually.

Choosing Between RIs and Savings Plans

Deciding between RIs and Savings Plans depends on your workload and usage patterns:

- **Predictable Workloads**: If you have stable and predictable workloads with specific instance requirements, RIs can offer significant savings, especially with upfront payments.

- **Dynamic or Variable Workloads**: If your workloads are dynamic or vary in instance type and region, Savings Plans provide more flexibility and may lead to better cost savings.

- **Convertible RIs**: Convertible RIs offer flexibility similar to Savings Plans, making them suitable for workloads with changing requirements.

- **Combining Both**: Some organizations use a combination of RIs and Savings Plans to maximize cost savings for different parts of their infrastructure.

Monitoring and Optimization

To effectively utilize RIs and Savings Plans, it's essential to continuously monitor your usage, review cost and usage reports, and make adjustments as needed. AWS provides tools like AWS Cost Explorer and AWS Trusted Advisor to help you analyze and optimize your spending.

By strategically using Reserved Instances and Savings Plans based on your workload and usage characteristics, you can achieve significant cost savings while maintaining the flexibility to adapt to changing requirements in your AWS environment.

Section 11.5: Cost Optimization Best Practices

Cost optimization is an ongoing process in your AWS environment. To ensure that you're making the most of your resources while controlling expenses, consider the following best practices:

1. Tag Your Resources

Tagging your AWS resources is essential for cost allocation and tracking. Assign meaningful tags to resources such as EC2 instances, S3 buckets, and RDS databases. Tags help you identify the owner, project, or purpose of each resource, making it easier to allocate costs to the right teams or departments.

Here's an example of tagging EC2 instances using the AWS CLI:

aws ec2 create-tags—resources i-1234567890abcdef0—tags Key=Environment,Value=Production Key=Owner,Value=JohnDoe

2. Rightsize Your Resources

Regularly analyze your resource utilization and adjust instance sizes accordingly. AWS offers tools like AWS Trusted Advisor and AWS Cost Explorer to help you identify underutilized or oversized instances. Downsizing or using the appropriate instance type can lead to significant cost savings.

3. Implement Auto Scaling

Utilize AWS Auto Scaling to automatically adjust the number of instances based on demand. Auto Scaling ensures you have the right capacity to handle your workloads without over-provisioning, which can result in unnecessary costs.

4. Leverage Spot Instances

For fault-tolerant and flexible workloads, consider using Amazon EC2 Spot Instances. These instances offer substantial cost savings compared to on-demand pricing. Spot Instances allow you to use spare EC2 capacity at a lower price.

5. Monitor and Analyze Cost and Usage

AWS provides several cost management and monitoring tools. Use Amazon CloudWatch to gain insights into your resource utilization and set up alarms for cost thresholds. AWS Cost Explorer helps you visualize and understand your spending patterns.

6. Embrace Serverless Computing

AWS Lambda and other serverless services allow you to pay only for the compute resources you use, with no upfront costs. Serverless architectures can be highly cost-effective for event-driven workloads.

7. Implement Data Lifecycle Policies

For data stored in Amazon S3, Glacier, or EBS, set up data lifecycle policies. Automatically transition data to lower-cost storage tiers or delete obsolete data based on predefined rules.

8. Review and Modify Reservations

Regularly review your Reserved Instances and Savings Plans to ensure they match your current workload requirements. Modify or purchase new reservations as needed to avoid underutilization or overspending.

9. Monitor and Optimize Databases

Optimize your database resources by choosing the right instance type, enabling automated backups and snapshots, and using Amazon RDS Performance Insights to identify and resolve performance bottlenecks.

10. Implement Cost Controls

Leverage AWS Budgets and Cost and Usage Reports to set cost controls and spending limits. Establish alerts to notify you when costs exceed predefined thresholds.

11. Educate Your Team

Ensure that your AWS team is aware of cost optimization best practices. AWS offers training and certification programs to help your team build expertise in managing costs effectively.

12. Explore AWS Trusted Advisor

AWS Trusted Advisor provides recommendations for optimizing costs, security, performance, and fault tolerance. Regularly review Trusted Advisor's cost optimization recommendations to identify potential savings opportunities.

By following these cost optimization best practices and regularly reviewing your AWS environment for opportunities to reduce expenses, you can maximize the value of your AWS investment while keeping costs under control. Cost optimization is an ongoing effort, and with the right strategies in place, you can achieve a balance between performance and cost-effectiveness in the cloud.

Chapter 12: AWS DevOps and CI/CD

Section 12.1: Continuous Integration and Continuous Deployment (CI/CD)

Continuous Integration and Continuous Deployment (CI/CD) are essential practices for modern software development and deployment. CI/CD pipelines automate the process of building, testing, and deploying applications, resulting in faster and more reliable releases. In this section, we'll explore the concepts of CI/CD and how AWS services can facilitate the implementation of CI/CD pipelines.

What is CI/CD?

CI/CD is a software development practice that focuses on automating and streamlining the steps involved in software delivery. It consists of two main phases:

1. **Continuous Integration (CI):** In this phase, code changes from multiple developers are frequently integrated into a shared repository. Each integration triggers automated builds and tests to catch and fix issues early.
2. **Continuous Deployment (CD):** After successful CI, the CD phase automates the deployment of the application to various environments, such as development, staging, and production. This automation ensures that code changes are consistently deployed and that the application is always in a deployable state.

Benefits of CI/CD on AWS

Implementing CI/CD pipelines on AWS offers several advantages:

1. **Faster Development:** CI/CD automates time-consuming tasks, reducing manual intervention and accelerating the development cycle.
2. **Quality Assurance:** Automated testing in CI/CD pipelines improves code quality by catching bugs and issues early in the development process.
3. **Consistency:** CD ensures that applications are deployed consistently across different environments, reducing configuration drift and minimizing deployment-related errors.
4. **Scalability:** AWS provides scalable resources and services, making it easier to build and deploy applications with varying workloads.

AWS CI/CD Services

AWS offers a range of services to support CI/CD pipelines:

- **AWS CodePipeline:** A fully managed CI/CD service that automates the building, testing, and deployment of code changes. CodePipeline integrates with other AWS services and third-party tools to create flexible pipelines.

- **AWS CodeBuild:** A fully managed build service that compiles source code, runs tests, and produces software packages. It integrates seamlessly with CodePipeline and supports various programming languages and build tools.

- **AWS CodeDeploy:** Automates code deployments to a variety of compute resources, including EC2 instances, Lambda functions, and on-premises servers. CodeDeploy ensures that deployments are consistent and reliable.

- **AWS CodeCommit:** A managed source code control service that hosts Git repositories. It allows teams to collaborate on code and integrates with other AWS CI/CD services.

- **AWS CodeArtifact:** A secure, scalable, and fully managed artifact repository that makes it easy to store, publish, and share software packages. It integrates with other AWS DevOps services and popular build tools.

- **AWS CodeStar:** A fully managed development service that provides a unified user interface for developing, building, and deploying applications on AWS. It supports various programming languages and frameworks.

- **AWS Elastic Beanstalk:** A platform as a service (PaaS) offering that simplifies application deployment, monitoring, and scaling. It supports multiple programming languages and web frameworks.

In the following sections, we'll delve deeper into each of these services, exploring how to set up CI/CD pipelines, automate builds, and deploy applications on AWS. Implementing CI/CD practices using these services can help you achieve faster, more reliable, and consistent software delivery.

Section 12.2: AWS CodePipeline

AWS CodePipeline is a fully managed continuous integration and continuous deployment (CI/CD) service that automates the end-to-end software release process. It allows you to build, test, and deploy your code changes quickly and reliably. CodePipeline enables you to define a series of stages and actions that your code goes through, from source code repositories to deployment to production. In this section, we will explore AWS CodePipeline and its key features.

Key Concepts of AWS CodePipeline

Pipeline:

- A pipeline is the core construct of CodePipeline. It represents a series of stages and actions that your code goes through during the release process.

Stage:

- A stage is a logical collection of one or more actions. For example, you might have a "Build" stage and a "Deploy" stage in your pipeline.

Action:

- An action represents a task within a stage, such as building code, running tests, or deploying to a specific environment. Each action is associated with a provider, such as AWS CodeBuild or AWS CodeDeploy.

Source Stage:

- The source stage retrieves the source code from your chosen source repository, such as AWS CodeCommit, GitHub, or Amazon S3.

Build Stage:

- The build stage compiles your source code and runs tests. AWS CodeBuild is commonly used for this purpose.

Deploy Stage:

- The deploy stage deploys your application to a specific environment, such as an Amazon EC2 instance or an AWS Lambda function. AWS CodeDeploy is often used for deployments.

Artifact:

- An artifact is a collection of files produced as the output of a build or test action. Artifacts are passed between stages to ensure consistency.

Benefits of AWS CodePipeline

Automation:

- CodePipeline automates the entire release process, reducing the risk of human error and ensuring consistency in your deployments.

Flexibility:

- You can define custom stages and actions to suit your specific requirements, making CodePipeline highly adaptable.

Integration:

- CodePipeline integrates seamlessly with other AWS services like AWS CodeBuild, AWS CodeDeploy, and AWS Lambda, as well as third-party tools.

Monitoring:

- CodePipeline provides real-time visibility into your pipeline's status and execution history, making it easy to diagnose and troubleshoot issues.

Creating a Basic CodePipeline

Here's a high-level overview of how to create a basic CodePipeline:

1. **Create a CodePipeline:** In the AWS Management Console, navigate to CodePipeline and create a new pipeline. Specify the source repository, build, and deployment settings.
2. **Define Stages and Actions:** Configure the stages and actions that make up your pipeline. For example, you might have a "Source" stage that pulls code from CodeCommit, a "Build" stage that uses CodeBuild, and a "Deploy" stage that utilizes CodeDeploy.
3. **Configure Artifacts:** Specify how artifacts are passed between stages. This ensures that the output of one stage becomes the input for the next.
4. **Review and Create:** Review your pipeline configuration, and create the pipeline.
5. **Start Your Pipeline:** Your pipeline can be triggered manually or automatically whenever changes are made to your source repository.

Example CodePipeline Workflow

Here's an example workflow of a CodePipeline for a web application:

1. **Source Stage:**

    – Code is retrieved from a GitHub repository.
    – An artifact is created with the source code.

1. **Build Stage:**

    – AWS CodeBuild compiles the source code, runs tests, and generates a deployable artifact.

1. **Deploy Stage (Staging):**

    – AWS CodeDeploy deploys the artifact to a staging environment for testing.

1. **Manual Approval Stage:**

    – An optional manual approval stage allows human intervention for quality assurance.

1. **Deploy Stage (Production):**

    – After approval, AWS CodeDeploy deploys the artifact to the production environment.

By using AWS CodePipeline, you can automate this workflow, ensuring that code changes are thoroughly tested in a staging environment before being deployed to production. This improves code quality and reduces the risk of deployment errors.

In the next sections, we will explore other AWS DevOps services that complement AWS CodePipeline to create robust CI/CD pipelines for your applications.

Section 12.3: AWS CodeBuild

AWS CodeBuild is a fully managed continuous integration service that compiles source code, runs tests, and produces software packages that are ready for deployment. It's a fundamental component of the CI/CD (Continuous Integration and Continuous Deployment) pipeline, working alongside services like AWS CodePipeline and AWS CodeDeploy to automate software release processes. In this section, we'll delve into the key concepts and features of AWS CodeBuild.

Key Concepts of AWS CodeBuild

Build Project:

- A build project is a configuration for running a build in CodeBuild. It specifies the build environment, source code location, build commands, and other settings. You can create multiple build projects for different applications or components.

Build Environment:

- CodeBuild offers various pre-configured build environments, including popular programming languages and build tools. You can also create custom build environments tailored to your specific requirements.

Source Code Repository:

- CodeBuild can pull source code from various repositories, including AWS CodeCommit, GitHub, Bitbucket, and Amazon S3.

Build Spec:

- A build spec is a YAML or JSON file that defines the build phases, commands, and post-build actions. It provides fine-grained control over the build process.

Artifacts:

- CodeBuild produces artifacts as the build output. These artifacts can include compiled binaries, libraries, and other files necessary for deployment.

Benefits of AWS CodeBuild

Scalability:

- CodeBuild can scale automatically to handle a high volume of builds, ensuring quick feedback for developers.

Managed Build Environments:

- AWS provides a range of managed build environments with popular build tools and languages pre-installed, reducing the need for custom configurations.

Integration:

- CodeBuild seamlessly integrates with other AWS services like CodePipeline and CodeDeploy, making it an integral part of your CI/CD pipeline.

Security:

- Build environments can run in isolated Amazon EC2 instances, enhancing security by preventing cross-contamination between builds.

Pay-as-You-Go Pricing:

- With CodeBuild's pay-as-you-go pricing model, you only pay for the compute resources used during the build, making it cost-effective.

Creating a CodeBuild Project

Here's an overview of how to create a CodeBuild project:

1. **Define the Source:** Specify the source code location, which can be an AWS CodeCommit repository, GitHub repository, Bitbucket repository, or an Amazon S3 bucket.
2. **Choose the Build Environment:** Select a pre-configured build environment or create a custom one tailored to your needs. You can choose the programming language, build tools, and runtime versions.
3. **Configure the Build Spec:** Create a build spec file (buildspec.yml) that defines the build phases, commands, and post-build actions. This file provides complete control over the build process.

4. **Set Up Artifacts:** Specify the artifacts that should be generated as the build output. You can publish them to an S3 bucket, Amazon ECR (Elastic Container Registry), or other destinations.
5. **Define IAM Roles:** Ensure that the CodeBuild service has the necessary permissions to access your source code repository, build environment, and other AWS resources.
6. **Start a Build:** Trigger the build manually or automatically whenever changes are pushed to the source code repository.

Example Build Project

Suppose you have a Node.js application stored in a GitHub repository. You want to create a CodeBuild project to build and test this application. Here are the steps:

1. **Source Configuration:**

- Specify the GitHub repository URL and branch.
- Provide access credentials if required.

1. **Build Environment:**

- Choose a Node.js build environment with the desired Node.js version.
- Configure environment variables if needed.

1. **Build Spec:**

- Create a buildspec.yml file with the necessary build commands, such as installing dependencies, running tests, and packaging the application.

1. **Artifacts:**

– Specify that the build artifacts should be stored in an S3 bucket.

1. **IAM Roles:**

– Ensure that the CodeBuild service role has permissions to access GitHub and upload artifacts to S3.

1. **Start a Build:**

– Trigger the build manually or set up a webhook to start the build automatically when code changes are pushed to GitHub.

AWS CodeBuild simplifies the process of building and testing code, helping teams deliver high-quality software quickly and reliably. When combined with AWS CodePipeline and AWS CodeDeploy, you can create a comprehensive CI/CD pipeline that automates the entire software release process.

Section 12.4: AWS CodeDeploy

AWS CodeDeploy is a deployment service that automates the process of deploying applications to a variety of compute services such as Amazon EC2 instances, AWS Fargate, Lambda functions, and even on-premises servers. It allows you to consistently and reliably deploy your applications, making it a critical component of a CI/CD (Continuous Integration and Continuous Deployment) pipeline. In this section, we'll explore the key concepts and features of AWS CodeDeploy.

Key Concepts of AWS CodeDeploy

Application:

- An application in CodeDeploy represents the code that you want to deploy. It can consist of multiple revisions, each of which represents a version of your application code.

Deployment Group:

- A deployment group is a set of Amazon EC2 instances, AWS Fargate tasks, or Lambda functions that you target for a deployment. You can create different deployment groups for various environments like development, testing, and production.

Deployment Configuration:

- Deployment configurations define how deployments are conducted. They specify options such as the percentage of instances to be updated at once, the order of deployment, and error handling behavior.

Revision:

- A revision is a specific version of your application code, bundled with deployment artifacts such as executables, scripts, and configuration files.

Deployment:

- A deployment is the process of taking a revision and deploying it to a deployment group. It can be initiated manually or automatically as part of a CI/CD pipeline.

Deployment Strategies

AWS CodeDeploy supports several deployment strategies to control the rollout of new code versions. Some of the commonly used strategies include:

- **In-Place Deployment:** The new version of the application replaces the existing one on each instance or server. This is suitable for applications that can't have multiple versions running simultaneously.

- **Blue/Green Deployment:** This strategy provisions a new set of instances (the "green" environment) and deploys the new version there. After testing, traffic is gradually shifted from the old (blue) environment to the new one. This approach allows for quick rollbacks if issues are detected.

- **Canary Deployment:** In this strategy, a small subset of instances receives the new code first (the "canaries"). After monitoring the canaries for issues, the deployment is expanded to more instances. This approach is useful for minimizing the impact of potential issues.

Benefits of AWS CodeDeploy

Flexibility:

- CodeDeploy supports various deployment targets, making it versatile for deploying applications on different compute services.

Integration:

- It seamlessly integrates with other AWS services, including AWS CodePipeline, AWS CodeBuild, and AWS Elastic Beanstalk, to create a robust CI/CD pipeline.

Rollback Capability:

- CodeDeploy allows you to quickly roll back deployments in case of issues or failures.

Agent-Based Deployment:

- It uses an agent installed on target instances, which can be EC2 instances, on-premises servers, or Lambda functions. This agent simplifies the deployment process.

Monitoring and Visibility:

- CodeDeploy provides detailed deployment logs and metrics to help you monitor and troubleshoot deployments.

Deploying with AWS CodeDeploy

Here's an overview of the steps to deploy an application using AWS CodeDeploy:

1. **Define an Application:** Create an application in CodeDeploy to represent your application code.
2. **Create a Deployment Group:** Define a deployment group that specifies the target environment, instances, or Lambda functions for the deployment.
3. **Package Your Application:** Bundle your application code and any required deployment artifacts into a revision.
4. **Create a Deployment:** Initiate a deployment by specifying the revision to deploy and the deployment group to target.
5. **Monitor and Troubleshoot:** Monitor the deployment progress using the CodeDeploy console, CloudWatch logs, and deployment logs.
6. **Rollback if Necessary:** If issues are detected during deployment, you can easily roll back to a previous version.

Example Deployment

Suppose you have a web application running on Amazon EC2 instances and want to deploy a new version using AWS CodeDeploy. Here are the steps:

1. **Define an Application:**

– Create an application in CodeDeploy, e.g., "MyWebApp."

1. **Create a Deployment Group:**

– Define a deployment group, e.g., "ProductionDeploymentGroup," that specifies the EC2 instances where you want to deploy.

1. **Package Your Application:**

– Bundle your new application code and configuration files into a revision package.

1. **Create a Deployment:**

– Initiate a deployment to the "ProductionDeploymentGroup" using the revision package.

1. **Monitor and Troubleshoot:**

– Monitor the deployment progress in the CodeDeploy console and check CloudWatch logs for any errors.

1. **Rollback if Necessary:**

– If issues arise, you can quickly roll back to the previous version by creating a new deployment with the previous revision.

AWS CodeDeploy simplifies the deployment process, making it easier to maintain and update your applications while ensuring minimal downtime and reducing deployment errors. When integrated into a comprehensive CI/CD pipeline, it becomes a powerful tool for achieving continuous delivery of software.

Section 12.5: Serverless CI/CD with AWS

Lambda

Serverless computing has revolutionized the way applications are built and deployed. In this section, we'll explore how you can implement a serverless Continuous Integration and Continuous Deployment (CI/CD) pipeline using AWS Lambda and other AWS services.

Benefits of Serverless CI/CD

Serverless CI/CD offers several advantages:

Cost-Efficiency:

- You pay only for the execution time of your CI/CD pipeline, which can result in cost savings compared to maintaining dedicated CI/CD servers.

Scalability:

- Serverless CI/CD can automatically scale to handle increased workloads, ensuring your pipeline remains responsive even during peak times.

Simplified Maintenance:

- There's no need to manage and patch CI/CD server infrastructure, reducing administrative overhead.

Speed:

- Serverless CI/CD can execute tasks concurrently, speeding up your build and deployment processes.

Components of Serverless CI/CD

AWS Lambda:

- AWS Lambda is at the core of serverless CI/CD. It allows you to execute code in response to events. In this case, Lambda functions are used to run your CI/CD pipeline tasks.

Amazon S3:

- Amazon S3 can store your application code, build artifacts, and deployment scripts. It serves as a central repository for your CI/CD pipeline.

AWS CodePipeline:

- AWS CodePipeline is a fully managed CI/CD service that orchestrates the steps of your pipeline. It integrates with Lambda functions, S3, and other AWS services.

AWS CodeBuild:

- AWS CodeBuild can build and package your application code. It integrates seamlessly with CodePipeline.

AWS CodeDeploy:

- AWS CodeDeploy can be used to automate deployments to your target environment, whether it's EC2 instances, Lambda functions, or other AWS services.

Implementing a Serverless CI/CD Pipeline

Here's an outline of how to set up a serverless CI/CD pipeline:

1. **Define Your Pipeline Stages:**

- Identify the stages of your pipeline, such as source code retrieval, build, test, and deployment.

1. **Create Lambda Functions:**

- Develop Lambda functions for each stage of your pipeline. For example, you might have a function that retrieves source code from a version control system, another for building the code, and another for deploying it.

1. **Configure AWS CodePipeline:**

- Set up a CodePipeline and define the stages and actions. Integrate your Lambda functions into the pipeline.

1. **Store Artifacts in Amazon S3:**

- Use Amazon S3 to store build artifacts, application code, and deployment scripts. Your Lambda functions can access these resources.

1. **Implement CI/CD Logic:**

- Write the logic in your Lambda functions to perform the necessary tasks, such as fetching source code, running tests, and deploying the application.

1. **Trigger Pipeline on Code Changes:**

– Configure CodePipeline to automatically trigger when changes are pushed to your version control system, such as AWS CodeCommit or GitHub.

1. **Monitoring and Error Handling:**

– Implement logging and error handling in your Lambda functions to capture and troubleshoot any issues that may arise during the pipeline execution.

1. **Testing and Validation:**

– Thoroughly test your serverless CI/CD pipeline to ensure it functions correctly. Test different scenarios, including successful builds and deployments as well as failure cases.

1. **Scaling Considerations:**

– Design your pipeline to scale as needed. Lambda functions can be configured to handle concurrent executions, and you can adjust their memory and timeout settings based on your requirements.

1. **Security Best Practices:**

– Follow AWS security best practices to secure your CI/ CD pipeline. Use AWS Identity and Access Management (IAM) roles and policies to control access to AWS resources.

Example Serverless CI/CD Workflow

Here's a simplified example of a serverless CI/CD workflow using AWS services:

1. Developers commit code changes to a Git repository hosted on AWS CodeCommit.
2. AWS CodePipeline detects the changes and triggers the pipeline.
3. The pipeline invokes a Lambda function that retrieves the source code from CodeCommit.
4. Another Lambda function is triggered to build the application using AWS CodeBuild.
5. If the build is successful, the pipeline triggers a Lambda function for deployment using AWS CodeDeploy.
6. The Lambda function deploys the application to an Amazon EC2 Auto Scaling group.
7. Monitoring and logging Lambda functions capture and report pipeline execution details.

This serverless CI/CD approach provides an efficient and scalable way to automate your software development and deployment processes while minimizing operational overhead and costs. It's well-suited for modern, cloud-native applications that leverage serverless computing paradigms.

Chapter 13: Serverless Computing with AWS

Section 13.1: Introduction to Serverless Architecture

Serverless computing is a cloud computing model that allows you to build and run applications without managing the underlying server infrastructure. In a serverless architecture, cloud providers like AWS automatically allocate and manage the server resources needed to execute your code, scaling them up or down as necessary. This approach offers several benefits, including reduced operational overhead, cost savings, and improved scalability.

Key Concepts of Serverless Architecture

1. Event-Driven Execution:

- Serverless functions are event-driven, meaning they are triggered by specific events, such as HTTP requests, file uploads, database changes, or scheduled tasks. When an event occurs, the associated function is executed.

2. Stateless Functions:

- Serverless functions are stateless, meaning they don't maintain any persistent state between invocations. Each execution is independent, and data is typically stored externally, such as in a database or object storage.

3. Automatic Scaling:

• Cloud providers automatically scale the serverless environment based on the incoming workload. Functions can handle multiple concurrent executions, and you're only billed for the actual compute time used.

4. Pay-as-You-Go Pricing:

• Serverless computing follows a pay-as-you-go pricing model. You're charged based on the number of executions and the execution time, making it cost-effective for workloads with varying demand.

Advantages of Serverless Architecture

1. Reduced Management Overhead:

• With serverless, you don't need to provision, configure, or manage servers. Cloud providers handle infrastructure management, including server patching and scaling.

2. Cost Savings:

• Serverless eliminates the need to pay for idle server capacity. You only pay for the actual compute time, making it cost-efficient.

3. Scalability:

- Serverless functions can automatically scale to accommodate increased traffic, ensuring your application remains responsive.

4. Rapid Development:

- Serverless allows developers to focus on writing code rather than managing infrastructure, leading to faster development cycles.

AWS Lambda: AWS Serverless Compute Service

AWS Lambda is a popular serverless compute service provided by AWS. It allows you to run code in response to various events, such as HTTP requests, changes to data in Amazon S3, or updates to database records in Amazon DynamoDB. Lambda functions are stateless, and you can write them in languages like Python, Node.js, Java, and more.

Here's a simple example of a Lambda function written in Node.js:

```javascript
exports.handler = async (event) => {
// Your code logic here
const response = {
statusCode: 200,
body: JSON.stringify('Hello from Lambda!'),
};
return response;
};
```

In this example, the Lambda function responds with a "Hello from Lambda!" message when triggered.

Serverless architecture, with AWS Lambda as a core component, is particularly well-suited for building microservices, event-driven applications, real-time data processing, and APIs. It offers developers the flexibility to build and deploy applications quickly while benefiting from automatic scaling and cost savings.

In the following sections, we will explore various aspects of serverless computing with AWS Lambda and how to design and build serverless applications effectively.

Section 13.2: AWS Lambda Functions

AWS Lambda functions are at the heart of serverless computing on AWS. These functions allow you to run code in response to various events without having to manage the underlying infrastructure. In this section, we'll delve deeper into Lambda functions, discussing their characteristics, use cases, and how to create and configure them.

Key Characteristics of AWS Lambda Functions

1. **Event-Driven Execution:** Lambda functions are event-driven, meaning they are triggered by specific events or changes in AWS services. For example, a Lambda function can be triggered by an HTTP request via Amazon API Gateway, a new object being uploaded to an S3 bucket, or a record being added to an Amazon DynamoDB table.

2. **Stateless:** Lambda functions are stateless, which means they don't maintain any persistent state between executions. Each invocation of a Lambda function is independent, and any data that needs to persist should be stored in external data stores like databases or S3.

3. **Automatic Scaling:** AWS Lambda automatically scales the execution environment to handle incoming events. If your function experiences a sudden spike in requests, AWS

Lambda will provision additional resources to accommodate the load, ensuring that your application remains responsive.

4. **Pay-as-You-Go Pricing:** Lambda functions follow a pay-as-you-go pricing model. You are charged based on the number of executions and the duration of each execution. This cost-effective approach means you only pay for the compute resources you consume.

Use Cases for AWS Lambda

Lambda functions are versatile and can be used in a wide range of use cases, including:

• **APIs and Web Applications:** Lambda can power the backend of web applications and APIs, responding to HTTP requests. When combined with Amazon API Gateway, it provides a serverless API solution.

• **Data Processing:** Lambda functions are ideal for processing data, such as image or video transcoding, log processing, and ETL (Extract, Transform, Load) jobs.

• **Real-time File Processing:** When files are uploaded to an S3 bucket, Lambda can automatically trigger processing tasks, such as resizing images or extracting metadata.

• **IoT and Event-Driven Applications:** AWS IoT events or custom events can trigger Lambda functions to respond to changes in device states or custom application events.

- **Scheduled Tasks:** Lambda functions can be scheduled to run at specific intervals, making them suitable for tasks like generating reports, cleaning up resources, and sending notifications.

Creating and Configuring Lambda Functions

To create a Lambda function, you need to define its runtime, such as Node.js, Python, or Java, and specify the execution role that grants necessary permissions to access AWS resources. You can also configure environment variables, set up triggers, and define the function's code and handler.

Here's a simplified example of a Lambda function in Python:

```python
import json
def lambda_handler(event, context):
# Your code logic here
response = {
"statusCode": 200,
"body": json.dumps("Hello from Lambda!")
}
return response
```

In this example, the lambda_handler function responds with a "Hello from Lambda!" message.

In the subsequent sections, we will explore more advanced Lambda function configurations, best practices for development and deployment, and how to integrate them with other AWS services to build serverless applications.

Section 13.3: Building Serverless APIs with API Gateway

Amazon API Gateway is a fully managed service that makes it easy to create, publish, and manage APIs for serverless applications. In this section, we'll explore how to use API Gateway to build serverless APIs that integrate with AWS Lambda functions.

Key Concepts of Amazon API Gateway

1. APIs and Resources:

- In API Gateway, an API is a collection of resources and methods. Resources represent entities like objects, and methods define how you interact with these resources (e.g., GET, POST, PUT).

- For example, you might have an API for managing products, where /products is a resource, and GET, POST, PUT, and DELETE are methods.

2. Stages:

- An API Gateway API can have multiple stages, such as dev, test, and prod. Stages allow you to deploy different versions of your API.

- Stages also provide a stable URL for accessing your API, like https://api.example.com/prod.

3. Deployments:

- A deployment is a snapshot of your API at a specific point in time. You can create multiple deployments for the same API to manage different versions.

- Deployments are associated with stages and are used to make your API changes live.

4. API Gateway Authorizers:

- Authorizers are used to control access to your API by authenticating users or applications. You can use Amazon Cognito, IAM, or custom authorizers.

5. Mapping Templates:

- Mapping templates transform incoming request data and outgoing response data to and from JSON or other formats.

- They are often used to convert input data to a format that your Lambda function expects and to format the response.

Building a Simple API with API Gateway and Lambda

Here's a step-by-step guide to building a simple API using API Gateway and Lambda:

1. Create a Lambda Function:

– Begin by creating a Lambda function that will handle API requests. You can write your Lambda function code in your preferred language (e.g., Node.js, Python, Java).

1. Create an API in API Gateway:

– In the API Gateway console, create a new API. You can choose a REST API or HTTP API, depending on your requirements.

1. **Define Resources and Methods:**

– Add resources and methods to your API. For example, you might create a /products resource with GET, POST, PUT, and DELETE methods.

1. **Integrate with Lambda:**

– Configure the methods to integrate with your Lambda function. You'll need to specify the Lambda function's ARN (Amazon Resource Name).

1. **Deploy Your API:**

– Create a deployment and associate it with a stage (e.g., prod). Deployments make your API changes live and provide a stable URL.

1. **Test Your API:**

– Use the provided URL to test your API using tools like curl, Postman, or browser-based REST clients.

1. **Set Up Authorization (Optional):**

– If your API requires authentication, configure authorizers to control access.

1. **Monitoring and Scaling:**

– Use API Gateway features like logging, monitoring, and throttling to ensure your API operates smoothly.

API Gateway simplifies the process of creating and managing APIs, making it an essential component of serverless architectures for building scalable and secure web services. In the next sections, we will explore advanced features of API Gateway and how to secure and optimize your serverless APIs.

Section 13.4: Event-Driven Serverless Applications

Event-driven serverless applications are a powerful way to build responsive, scalable, and cost-effective systems that respond to events and triggers. In this section, we'll explore the concept of event-driven architecture and how AWS Lambda, Amazon S3, Amazon SQS, and Amazon EventBridge can be used to create such applications.

Event-Driven Architecture Overview

Event-driven architecture is a software design pattern where the flow of the application is determined by events, such as user actions, system events, or data changes. Events are generated and consumed by different components of the system, allowing them to communicate asynchronously.

Key characteristics of event-driven architecture include:

1. **Decoupling:** Components are decoupled, meaning they don't need to know about each other. They communicate through events.
2. **Scalability:** Event-driven systems can easily scale because new components can be added to handle increased event loads.
3. **Resilience:** If a component fails, events can be replayed, ensuring that no data is lost.
4. **Flexibility:** New functionality can be added by simply

connecting components to existing event streams.

AWS Services for Event-Driven Architectures

AWS offers several services that are essential for building event-driven serverless applications:

1. AWS Lambda:

- Lambda is a serverless compute service that can execute code in response to events. It can be triggered by various AWS services or custom events.

2. Amazon S3:

- Amazon S3 can generate events when objects are created, updated, or deleted in a bucket. These events can trigger Lambda functions, allowing you to process data automatically.

3. Amazon SQS (Simple Queue Service):

- SQS provides a scalable and fully managed message queue service. It can be used to decouple components and distribute workloads.

4. Amazon EventBridge:

- EventBridge is a serverless event bus service that makes it easy to connect different applications using events. It can route events from various sources to Lambda functions or other targets.

Building an Event-Driven Application

Let's consider a simple example of building an event-driven image processing application:

1. **Upload Image to S3:**

– When a user uploads an image to an S3 bucket, S3 generates an event.

1. **Trigger Lambda Function:**

– Configure an S3 event trigger that invokes a Lambda function whenever a new image is uploaded.

1. **Image Processing:**

– The Lambda function can process the image, generate thumbnails, and perform other tasks.

1. **Publish Event:**

– After processing, the Lambda function can publish an event to an event bus (e.g., Amazon EventBridge).

1. **Other Components Respond:**

– Other Lambda functions or services can subscribe to this event and take further actions, such as sending notifications or storing metadata.

1. **Scaling and Resilience:**

– The system can easily scale to handle more uploads, and if any component fails, the events can be replayed to ensure data integrity.

Benefits of Event-Driven Serverless Architectures

- **Scalability:** Event-driven architectures can scale horizontally, allowing your application to handle increasing workloads seamlessly.

- **Cost-Efficiency:** With serverless services like Lambda, you only pay for the compute time used during event processing.

- **Flexibility:** Components can be added or modified without affecting the entire system.

- **Resilience:** Event replay and error handling ensure that no events or data are lost.

- **Real-time Responsiveness:** Applications can respond to events in near real-time, providing a great user experience.

Event-driven serverless architectures are a fundamental building block for modern cloud-native applications. They enable you to build highly responsive and scalable systems while optimizing costs and simplifying development and maintenance. In the following section, we'll explore best practices and considerations for designing and deploying event-driven applications on AWS.

Section 13.5: Best Practices for Serverless Development

Serverless computing has become a popular paradigm for building scalable and cost-effective applications. However, to fully leverage the benefits of serverless, it's important to follow best practices. In this section, we'll explore key best practices for serverless development on AWS.

1. Right-Sizing Functions:

- Break down your application logic into small, focused Lambda functions. Avoid monolithic functions that perform multiple tasks. This allows for better scalability and cost optimization.

2. Use Triggers Efficiently:

- Choose the right event source (trigger) for your Lambda functions. Use event-driven triggers like S3 events, API Gateway, or Amazon EventBridge to invoke functions only when needed.

3. Manage Dependencies:

- Minimize the size of deployment packages by excluding unnecessary dependencies. Smaller packages lead to faster cold starts and reduced resource consumption.

4. Optimize Memory and Timeout:

- Adjust the memory allocation and timeout settings for your Lambda functions based on their resource requirements. This can impact performance and cost.

 # Example AWS SAM (Serverless Application Model) template
```
Resources:
MyFunction:
Type: AWS::Serverless::Function
Properties:
Handler: index.handler
MemorySize: 256
Timeout: 10
```

5. Concurrency and Throttling:

- Understand the concurrency limits and throttling behavior of AWS services you use, like DynamoDB and API Gateway. Implement retry mechanisms for transient failures.

6. Error Handling and Logging:

- Implement robust error handling in your functions. Use logging to capture relevant information for troubleshooting and monitoring. AWS CloudWatch Logs is a common choice.

7. Environment Variables:

- Store configuration and secrets as environment variables rather than hardcoding them in your code. AWS Secrets Manager and Systems Manager Parameter Store can help manage secrets.

 # Python Lambda function reading environment variables
```
import os
MY_SECRET = os.environ['MY_SECRET']
```

8. Security Best Practices:

• Apply AWS IAM (Identity and Access Management) policies to grant the least privilege necessary to functions. Use AWS Key Management Service (KMS) for encryption.

9. Testing and Deployment:

• Implement automated testing for your functions, including unit tests and integration tests. Use deployment tools like AWS SAM, Serverless Framework, or AWS CDK for infrastructure as code.

10. Monitoring and Observability:

- Set up comprehensive monitoring and alerting for your serverless applications. Use AWS CloudWatch Metrics, CloudWatch Alarms, and AWS X-Ray for tracing.

11. Cold Starts:

- Mitigate cold starts (initialization time) by using provisioned concurrency or warming strategies. Cold starts can impact the response time of your functions.

12. Cost Optimization:

- Continuously monitor and optimize costs. Leverage features like AWS Cost Explorer, AWS Budgets, and AWS Trusted Advisor to control expenses.

13. Documentation:

- Maintain up-to-date documentation for your serverless applications, including architecture diagrams and deployment instructions. This aids in onboarding and troubleshooting.

Serverless development offers numerous advantages, but it's important to be aware of these best practices to build robust, efficient, and secure applications. Following these guidelines will help you make the most of serverless technologies while avoiding common pitfalls. As serverless continues to evolve, staying informed about best practices is essential for successful cloud-native development.

Chapter 14: AWS Big Data and Analytics

Section 14.1: Amazon EMR (Elastic MapReduce)

Amazon EMR (Elastic MapReduce) is a cloud-native big data platform that simplifies processing vast amounts of data quickly and cost-effectively. It's designed to handle various data processing tasks, including batch processing, data transformation, and machine learning at scale. In this section, we'll explore Amazon EMR and how it can help you analyze and process large datasets on AWS.

What is Amazon EMR?

Amazon EMR is built on Apache Hadoop and other popular open-source frameworks like Apache Spark, Apache Hive, and Apache HBase. It provides an easy way to run big data frameworks without the complexities of managing infrastructure. With EMR, you can launch clusters of Amazon Elastic Compute Cloud (EC2) instances with pre-installed big data software and libraries.

Key Features of Amazon EMR:

1. **Scalability:** EMR allows you to start with small clusters and scale them horizontally as your data processing needs grow. You can also use Auto Scaling to automate cluster resizing based on demand.
2. **Cost Optimization:** EMR supports various instance types, including spot instances, to help reduce costs. It also offers features like instance fleets and On-Demand Capacity Reservations.

3. **Security:** You can leverage AWS Identity and Access Management (IAM) to control access to your EMR clusters and use encryption options for data security.
4. **Managed Hadoop Ecosystem:** EMR takes care of the heavy lifting when it comes to managing Hadoop components, so you can focus on your data and applications.
5. **Integration:** EMR seamlessly integrates with other AWS services, such as Amazon S3 for data storage and AWS Glue for data cataloging.

Use Cases for Amazon EMR:

- **Data Processing:** EMR is well-suited for processing large volumes of data, whether it's log analysis, ETL (Extract, Transform, Load) jobs, or data warehousing.

- **Machine Learning:** You can use EMR to run distributed machine learning algorithms on large datasets.

- **Real-Time Analytics:** EMR can be integrated with tools like Apache Kafka and Amazon Kinesis for real-time data processing and analytics.

Getting Started with Amazon EMR:

1. **Create a Cluster:** You can create an EMR cluster using the AWS Management Console, AWS CLI, or AWS SDKs. Specify the applications and configuration you need.
2. **Submit Jobs:** Once your cluster is running, you can submit jobs using various frameworks like Apache Spark or Apache Hive.
3. **Monitor and Debug:** EMR provides detailed monitoring

through Amazon CloudWatch and cluster logs for debugging.

4. **Terminate Cluster:** After completing your data processing tasks, you can terminate the cluster to avoid unnecessary costs.

 # AWS CLI command to create an EMR cluster

aws emr create-cluster—name "MyCluster"—release-label emr-6.5.0 \

—applications Name=Hadoop Name=Spark Name=Hive Name=HBase \

—instance-type m5.xlarge—instance-count 5—ec2-attributes KeyName=my-key-pair \

—use-default-roles

Amazon EMR is a powerful tool for big data processing and analytics on AWS. It simplifies the deployment and management of big data clusters, making it accessible to a wide range of users, from data engineers to data scientists. In the following sections, we'll dive deeper into specific use cases and best practices for leveraging Amazon EMR effectively in your data workflows.

Section 14.2: Amazon Athena

Amazon Athena is a serverless, interactive query service that allows you to analyze data in Amazon S3 using standard SQL queries. It's a powerful tool for performing ad-hoc analysis on large datasets without the need for complex ETL (Extract, Transform, Load) processes or managing infrastructure. In this section, we'll explore Amazon Athena and how it enables you to gain insights from your data stored in S3.

Key Features of Amazon Athena:

1. **Serverless:** Athena is entirely serverless, meaning you don't need to provision or manage any infrastructure. You only pay for the queries you run, making it a cost-effective solution.
2. **Schema-on-Read:** Athena uses schema-on-read, allowing you to run SQL queries on semi-structured or unstructured data in S3. You can define the schema when querying the data, making it highly flexible.
3. **Integration:** Athena seamlessly integrates with other AWS services like Amazon S3, AWS Glue, and Amazon QuickSight. You can use Glue for data cataloging and QuickSight for visualization.
4. **Performance:** Athena is optimized for query performance, with features like query caching and parallel processing. It can handle large datasets efficiently.
5. **Security:** You can control access to Athena using AWS IAM, and data in S3 can be encrypted for security.

How Amazon Athena Works:

1. **Data Catalog:** You start by creating a data catalog in AWS Glue or directly in Athena. The catalog defines the schema of your data.
2. **Query Execution:** You write SQL queries in the Athena console or using API calls. Athena parses these queries, optimizes them, and then executes them against the data in S3.
3. **Results Output:** Query results can be stored in a new S3 location or downloaded locally for further analysis.

Use Cases for Amazon Athena:

- **Log Analysis:** Athena is commonly used for analyzing log files stored in S3, helping you gain insights into application performance and user behavior.

- **Data Lake Analytics:** If you have a data lake in Amazon S3, Athena allows you to run SQL queries without the need to move data to a separate database.

- **Ad-Hoc Analysis:** Data analysts and data scientists can use Athena for ad-hoc exploration of data, enabling them to quickly answer business questions.

Getting Started with Amazon Athena:

1. **Set Up a Data Catalog:** Create a data catalog in AWS Glue or directly in Athena. Define tables and schemas for your data.
2. **Write SQL Queries:** Use the Athena Query Editor or any SQL client that supports JDBC/ODBC to write and execute SQL queries.
3. **Review Query History:** Athena maintains a query history, allowing you to review and rerun previous queries.
4. **Visualize Data:** Connect Athena to Amazon QuickSight to create visualizations and dashboards based on query results.

—*Example SQL query in Athena*
```
SELECT product_category, COUNT(*) AS total_count
FROM my_table
GROUP BY product_category
ORDER BY total_count DESC
```

Amazon Athena simplifies the process of querying data in Amazon S3, making it accessible to a wide range of users. Its serverless and schema-on-read architecture, combined with standard SQL support, makes it a valuable tool for data analysis and exploration. In the next section, we'll dive into Amazon Redshift Spectrum, another powerful analytics service on AWS.

Section 14.3: Amazon Redshift Spectrum

Amazon Redshift Spectrum is a powerful analytics service that extends Amazon Redshift's capabilities to query data stored in Amazon S3. It allows you to run complex SQL queries on vast amounts of data in your S3 data lake without the need for loading or transforming the data into Redshift tables. In this section, we'll explore the key features and use cases of Amazon Redshift Spectrum.

Key Features of Amazon Redshift Spectrum:

1. **Separation of Storage and Compute:** Redshift Spectrum separates compute resources from storage, which means you can scale your query processing independently. You pay only for the queries you run, making it cost-effective.
2. **Query Performance:** It uses a massively parallel processing (MPP) architecture to deliver fast query performance, even on large datasets. You can also take advantage of Redshift's query optimization features.
3. **Integration:** Redshift Spectrum seamlessly integrates with Amazon Redshift, allowing you to join data stored in S3 with data in your Redshift data warehouse. You can also use Amazon QuickSight for visualization.
4. **Data Formats:** It supports various data formats, including Parquet, ORC, Avro, and more, making it compatible with a wide range of data sources.

5. **Security:** You can enforce fine-grained access control using AWS IAM and VPC endpoints. Data in S3 can be encrypted for added security.

How Amazon Redshift Spectrum Works:

1. **Data Organization:** Your data in Amazon S3 should be organized in a columnar format using supported data formats like Parquet or ORC. The data should be partitioned for better query performance.
2. **External Tables:** In Redshift Spectrum, you define external tables that reference your S3 data. These tables have metadata about the data's location and structure but don't contain the actual data.
3. **SQL Queries:** You can write SQL queries in Amazon Redshift that reference both Redshift tables and external tables. Redshift Spectrum handles query execution for external tables by pushing down the query to S3.
4. **Query Results:** The query results can be seamlessly combined with data from your Redshift tables, allowing you to join and analyze data from multiple sources.

Use Cases for Amazon Redshift Spectrum:

• **Data Lake Integration:** Redshift Spectrum is ideal for integrating data stored in your S3 data lake with your Redshift data warehouse. This enables you to perform analytics on unified datasets.

• **Cost-Effective Analytics:** Since you pay only for the queries you run, Redshift Spectrum is cost-effective for ad-hoc and exploratory analytics on large datasets.

- **Complex Data Analysis:** It's suitable for running complex SQL queries, including joins and aggregations, on semi-structured or structured data in S3.

Getting Started with Amazon Redshift Spectrum:

1. **Set Up Redshift Spectrum:** Ensure your Redshift cluster is configured to use Spectrum, and set up IAM roles for access to S3.
2. **Define External Tables:** Create external tables in Redshift that reference your S3 data. Specify the data format, location, and schema.
3. **Write SQL Queries:** Write SQL queries in Redshift that involve both Redshift tables and external tables. Redshift Spectrum transparently handles the external data.

—*Example SQL query in Redshift Spectrum*

```
SELECT sales.date, sales.amount, products.product_name
FROM spectrum_sales AS sales
JOIN spectrum_products AS products ON sales.product_id = products.product_id
WHERE sales.date BETWEEN '2023-01-01' AND '2023-12-31'
```

Amazon Redshift Spectrum is a versatile tool for analyzing data in your S3 data lake using the familiar SQL language. It complements Amazon Redshift, making it easier to work with large-scale data analytics and data warehousing. In the next section, we'll explore AWS Glue, a fully managed ETL service that can be used to prepare and catalog data for analytics.

Section 14.4: AWS Glue

AWS Glue is a fully managed extract, transform, and load (ETL) service that simplifies the process of preparing and loading data for analytics. It helps you discover and catalog data from various sources, transform and clean the data, and make it available for analysis. In this section, we'll explore the key features and use cases of AWS Glue.

Key Features of AWS Glue:

1. **Data Catalog:** AWS Glue provides a centralized data catalog that stores metadata about your data sources, transformations, and targets. This catalog is used to track and manage your data assets.
2. **Data Discovery:** You can use AWS Glue Data Catalog to discover data across various AWS services, databases, and data lakes. It creates a unified view of your data, making it easier to work with.
3. **ETL Jobs:** AWS Glue allows you to create ETL jobs using Python or Scala that define how data should be transformed. It supports both batch and real-time data processing.
4. **Dynamic Schema Inference:** Glue can automatically infer the schema of your data, reducing the need for manual schema definition. This is especially useful for semi-structured data.
5. **Data Preparation:** You can use AWS Glue to clean, enrich, and transform your data. It supports various transformation operations, such as filtering, aggregating, and joining datasets.
6. **Serverless Execution:** Glue jobs run in a serverless environment, which means you don't need to provision or manage servers. AWS takes care of scaling and resource

allocation.

How AWS Glue Works:

1. **Data Cataloging:** You start by cataloging your data sources in the AWS Glue Data Catalog. This involves defining tables and schemas for your datasets.
2. **ETL Job Creation:** Next, you create ETL jobs in AWS Glue, specifying the source, target, and transformation logic. Glue supports visual job authoring or custom scripting in Python or Scala.
3. **Data Transformation:** Glue executes the ETL job, which involves extracting data from the source, applying transformations, and loading it into the target. The job can handle both batch and streaming data.
4. **Data Quality and Validation:** You can incorporate data quality checks and validation steps in your ETL jobs to ensure the data meets your criteria.
5. **Data Loading:** The transformed data is loaded into data warehouses, data lakes, or other analytics tools for further analysis and reporting.

Use Cases for AWS Glue:

• **Data Integration:** AWS Glue is used to integrate data from various sources, including databases, data lakes, and streaming platforms, into a unified data store.

• **Data Warehousing:** It prepares and loads data into data warehousing services like Amazon Redshift for business intelligence and analytics.

- **Data Lakes:** AWS Glue can be used to clean and catalog data in data lakes, making it accessible for analysis using tools like Amazon Athena or Amazon Redshift Spectrum.

- **Data Migration:** When migrating from on-premises data centers to the cloud, Glue simplifies the ETL process, ensuring data is transformed and loaded correctly.

- **Real-time Data Processing:** It supports real-time ETL for streaming data, enabling real-time analytics and dashboards.

Getting Started with AWS Glue:

1. **Create Data Catalog:** Start by creating a Data Catalog in AWS Glue and define tables and schemas for your data sources.
2. **Author ETL Jobs:** Use the AWS Glue Console or Glue Studio for visual job authoring. Alternatively, write custom ETL scripts in Python or Scala.
3. **Run ETL Jobs:** Execute your ETL jobs, monitor their progress, and view logs and metrics in the AWS Glue Console.

```python
# Example AWS Glue ETL Job (Python)
from awsglue.context import GlueContext
from pyspark.context import SparkContext
from awsglue.transforms import *
# Create GlueContext and SparkContext
sc = SparkContext()
glueContext = GlueContext(sc)
# Define source and target data
```

```
    source_data                                        =
glueContext.create_dynamic_frame.from_catalog(database="source_db",
table_name="source_table")
    target_data                                        =
glueContext.create_dynamic_frame.from_catalog(database="target_db",
table_name="target_table")
    # Apply transformations
    transformed_data = ApplyMapping.apply(frame=source_data,
mappings=[("source_col1", "string", "target_col1", "string")])
    # Write transformed data to the target
    glueContext.write_dynamic_frame.from_catalog(frame=transformed
database="target_db", table_name="target_table")
```

AWS Glue simplifies the ETL process, making it easier to prepare and transform data for analytics, machine learning, and other data-driven tasks. In the next section, we'll explore how AWS addresses the Internet of Things (IoT) with AWS IoT services.

Section 14.5: Data Lake and Analytics Solutions

Data lakes have become a critical component of modern data architecture, allowing organizations to store vast amounts of structured and unstructured data at scale. AWS offers a range of services and solutions to build, manage, and analyze data lakes effectively. In this section, we'll explore these AWS offerings for data lakes and analytics.

Amazon S3 as the Foundation

Amazon Simple Storage Service (Amazon S3) often serves as the foundation for building data lakes on AWS. It provides highly scalable, durable, and secure object storage. You can use S3 to store data in its native format, making it easy to ingest, store, and retrieve data.

Data Lake Architectures

AWS supports various data lake architectures, including:

1. **Single Data Lake**: In this approach, all data is stored in a single, central data lake on Amazon S3. This simplifies data management and access.
2. **Multi-Data Lake**: Large organizations or business units may have multiple data lakes. Each data lake can be isolated for security and compliance.

Data Ingestion

To populate your data lake, AWS offers several ingestion tools:

- **AWS DataSync**: For fast, secure data transfer from on-premises storage to Amazon S3.

- **AWS Snow Family**: For large-scale data migration via physical devices.

- **AWS Glue**: For ETL jobs that transform and load data into your data lake.

Data Cataloging

AWS Glue Data Catalog serves as a centralized metadata repository for your data lake. It provides a catalog of metadata, including schema information, which makes it easier to discover and query data.

Data Preparation

Once data is ingested, it often requires cleaning and transformation. AWS Glue, as mentioned earlier, offers ETL capabilities for this purpose. You can also use services like Amazon Athena for querying and Amazon Redshift Spectrum for data warehousing.

Analytics and Querying

For analyzing data in your data lake, you can use:

- **Amazon Athena**: An interactive query service to analyze data in Amazon S3 using SQL.

- **Amazon Redshift**: A fully managed data warehouse service for complex analytics and business intelligence.

- **AWS Glue ETL**: To prepare data for analytics or machine learning.

Data Lake Security

Securing your data lake is paramount. AWS provides robust security features such as:

- **Amazon S3 Access Control**: Use bucket policies and IAM roles to control access.

- **AWS Identity and Access Management (IAM)**: Define fine-grained access permissions.

- **Amazon Macie**: Automatically discover, classify, and protect sensitive data.

Data Lake Governance

AWS Lake Formation helps set up, secure, and manage your data lake. It automates many data management tasks and enforces fine-grained access controls.

Cost Optimization

To optimize costs, you can use:

- **Amazon S3 Object Tagging**: Apply tags for cost allocation and tracking.

- **Amazon S3 Object Lifecycle Policies**: Automate data archiving or deletion based on rules.

In conclusion, AWS provides a comprehensive set of services and solutions to build and manage data lakes at scale. These data lakes can serve as valuable assets for deriving insights, driving analytics, and supporting machine learning workloads. Proper planning, governance, and security are essential for successfully managing data lakes in AWS.

Chapter 15: IoT and AWS

Section 15.1: Internet of Things (IoT) Fundamentals

The Internet of Things (IoT) represents a paradigm shift in the way we interact with devices and data. It's a concept that refers to the interconnection of everyday objects to the internet, allowing them to send and receive data. These objects, often referred to as "things," can include anything from household appliances and wearable devices to industrial machinery and vehicles. IoT has gained significant traction in various industries, including healthcare, manufacturing, agriculture, and smart cities, due to its potential to improve efficiency, enhance decision-making, and create new business opportunities.

IoT Components

IoT systems typically consist of several key components:

1. **Devices or Sensors:** These are the physical objects or sensors that collect data. They can range from simple temperature sensors to complex cameras and industrial machinery equipped with various sensors.
2. **Connectivity:** IoT devices need a way to transmit data to the cloud or other devices. This can be achieved through various means, such as Wi-Fi, cellular networks, Bluetooth, or low-power wide-area networks (LPWANs).
3. **Data Processing:** The data collected by IoT devices often requires processing and analysis. Cloud platforms, edge computing devices, or dedicated IoT gateways are used to perform this processing.

4. **Cloud Services:** Cloud platforms like AWS provide the infrastructure and services needed to store, process, and analyze IoT data at scale. AWS IoT Core is a central service for managing IoT devices and data.

5. **Applications and Dashboards:** The insights gained from IoT data are typically visualized through applications and dashboards. These interfaces allow users to monitor and control IoT devices and make data-driven decisions.

Key IoT Use Cases

IoT has a wide range of applications across industries. Some notable use cases include:

- **Smart Home Automation:** IoT enables homeowners to control lighting, thermostats, security cameras, and appliances remotely through smartphones or voice assistants.

- **Industrial IoT (IIoT):** In manufacturing and industrial settings, IoT devices monitor equipment health, optimize production processes, and predict maintenance needs to reduce downtime.

- **Agriculture:** IoT sensors in agriculture collect data on soil moisture, weather conditions, and crop health, helping farmers make informed decisions about irrigation and crop management.

- **Healthcare:** IoT-enabled medical devices and wearables monitor patient health, track medication adherence, and transmit data to healthcare providers for remote monitoring.

- **Smart Cities:** IoT technologies are used in urban planning to manage traffic, reduce energy consumption, and enhance public safety through connected streetlights and surveillance cameras.

AWS IoT Services

Amazon Web Services offers a suite of services for building scalable and secure IoT applications:

- **AWS IoT Core:** A managed cloud service for connecting IoT devices to the cloud. It provides features for device management, data ingestion, and rules-based processing.

- **AWS IoT Greengrass:** Enables local compute, messaging, and data caching for IoT devices, allowing them to operate even when disconnected from the cloud.

- **AWS IoT Device Management:** Simplifies the onboarding, organization, and management of IoT devices at scale.

- **AWS IoT Analytics:** Provides tools for processing, storing, and analyzing IoT data to gain insights and create automated actions.

- **AWS IoT Events:** Detects and responds to events from IoT sensors and applications, allowing you to automate workflows based on real-time data.

IoT continues to evolve, and its integration with cloud computing platforms like AWS opens up new possibilities for innovation and digital transformation in various industries. In the following sections, we will delve deeper into specific AWS IoT services and practical IoT use cases.

Section 15.2: AWS IoT Core

AWS IoT Core is a foundational service for building IoT applications on Amazon Web Services. It provides secure and scalable communication between Internet of Things (IoT) devices and the cloud. AWS IoT Core allows you to connect, manage, and interact with IoT devices, collect and process data, and trigger actions based on device data and events. Let's explore the key features and concepts of AWS IoT Core.

Device Registry and Shadow

The device registry in AWS IoT Core acts as a database for storing information about your IoT devices, including device metadata and authentication certificates. Each device is uniquely identified and associated with an X.509 certificate or other authentication methods.

One essential concept related to device management is the **Device Shadow**. A device shadow is a JSON document that represents the current state of a device. It allows you to interact with a device's state without directly connecting to the device. Shadows are particularly useful for managing the state of offline or intermittent devices and enabling synchronization when they reconnect.

Here's an example of a device shadow document for a smart light bulb:

```
{
"state": {
"reported": {
"brightness": 75,
```

```
"power": "on"
},
"desired": {
"brightness": 50,
"power": "off"
}
}
}
```

In this example, the reported section represents the device's current state, while the desired section reflects the desired state you want to set. You can update the desired state, and AWS IoT Core will take care of synchronizing it with the actual device state when the device is online.

MQTT Protocol

AWS IoT Core uses the MQTT (Message Queuing Telemetry Transport) protocol for communication between devices and the cloud. MQTT is a lightweight and efficient protocol designed for constrained environments, making it well-suited for IoT applications. It enables bi-directional communication between devices and the cloud, allowing devices to publish messages (e.g., sensor data) and subscribe to topics to receive commands and updates.

Security and Authentication

Security is a top priority in IoT, and AWS IoT Core offers robust security features. Devices connect to AWS IoT Core using X.509 certificates, device certificates, or other authentication methods. Communication between devices and AWS IoT Core is encrypted using TLS (Transport Layer Security) to protect data in transit.

Fine-grained access control is achieved through AWS Identity and Access Management (IAM) policies and IoT policies. IAM policies allow you to control who can perform actions on IoT resources, while IoT policies enable you to specify which devices are allowed to perform specific actions.

Rules Engine

AWS IoT Core includes a Rules Engine that allows you to define rules to process incoming device data and trigger actions. You can use SQL-like queries to filter and transform data from MQTT messages and route it to various AWS services such as Amazon S3, AWS Lambda, Amazon DynamoDB, and more. For example, you can create a rule to store temperature sensor data in an S3 bucket or trigger a Lambda function when a specific event occurs.

Device Communication and Shadow APIs

AWS IoT Core provides APIs and SDKs for device communication and shadow operations. These APIs allow devices to connect to AWS IoT Core, publish and subscribe to MQTT topics, and interact with device shadows. AWS SDKs are available for various programming languages, making it easier to integrate IoT functionality into your applications.

Scalability and High Availability

AWS IoT Core is designed to scale with your IoT deployments. It can handle millions of concurrent connections from devices. The service is distributed across multiple Availability Zones (AZs) to ensure high availability and fault tolerance.

In summary, AWS IoT Core simplifies the development of IoT applications by providing essential services for managing devices, secure communication, and data processing. It forms the foundation for building scalable and reliable IoT solutions on AWS. In the following sections, we will explore more advanced IoT services and use cases provided by AWS.

Section 15.3: AWS Greengrass

AWS Greengrass is a service that extends AWS capabilities to the edge of the network, allowing you to run AWS Lambda functions on IoT devices and securely connect them to the cloud. Greengrass enables local processing, data caching, and offline operation for IoT devices, reducing latency and ensuring that devices can continue to operate even when they lose connectivity to the cloud. Let's delve into the key features and concepts of AWS Greengrass.

Core Devices and Groups

At the core of AWS Greengrass are **Core Devices**. These devices act as hubs for running AWS Lambda functions and managing communication with edge devices. Core Devices can be physical hardware or virtual machines running Greengrass Core Software.

Greengrass organizes devices into **Groups**, which are logical collections of devices with similar functionality. Each Group has its own configuration that includes which Lambda functions to run locally and how to communicate with the cloud. Groups are particularly useful for managing large-scale deployments where devices share common functionality or configurations.

Local Execution with AWS Lambda

AWS Greengrass allows you to deploy and run AWS Lambda functions on Core Devices. This enables you to process data locally on the edge, reducing the need to send all data to the cloud for processing. Lambda functions can be written in various programming languages and can interact with local resources, including sensors, actuators, and local storage.

Here's a simple example of a Python Lambda function that runs on a Greengrass Core Device to process sensor data:

```python
import greengrasssdk
client = greengrasssdk.client('iot-data')
def lambda_handler(event, context):
sensor_data = event['sensor_data']
# Process sensor_data locally
result = process_data(sensor_data)
# Publish result to the cloud
client.publish(topic='results', payload=result)
```

In this example, the Lambda function receives sensor data, processes it locally, and publishes the result to a cloud topic. This local processing reduces latency and bandwidth usage.

Device Shadows

AWS Greengrass also supports Device Shadows, similar to AWS IoT Core. Device Shadows allow you to maintain a synchronized state between devices and the cloud. This feature is valuable for ensuring that devices continue to operate as expected even when they are temporarily disconnected from the cloud.

Local Resources and Local Lambda Resources

Greengrass enables you to manage local resources on Core Devices, such as files and certificates, using Local Resources. These resources can be used by Lambda functions for various tasks.

Local Lambda Resources, on the other hand, are resources that are deployed with Lambda functions and can be used by those functions. For example, you can include machine learning models as Local Lambda Resources, allowing Lambda functions to perform local inferencing.

Stream Manager

AWS Greengrass Stream Manager is a feature that allows you to manage data streams on Core Devices. It provides capabilities for data ingestion, storage, and forwarding. Stream Manager helps you collect and manage data from various sources on the edge, making it available for local processing and cloud synchronization.

Greengrass ML Inference

For machine learning (ML) workloads, AWS Greengrass supports ML inference at the edge. You can deploy ML models to Core Devices and use them for inferencing on locally generated data. This is particularly useful for applications that require real-time decision-making based on ML models without relying on cloud connectivity.

AWS Greengrass offers a comprehensive set of features for extending AWS capabilities to the edge, enabling edge computing and IoT scenarios. By running AWS Lambda functions locally on Core Devices, managing device groups, and utilizing Device Shadows and local resources, you can build IoT applications that are both responsive and efficient. In the following sections, we will explore more IoT services and use cases provided by AWS.

Section 15.4: Device Management and Security

Device management and security are critical aspects of IoT solutions, and AWS IoT Core provides robust tools and features for managing and securing IoT devices. In this section, we'll explore some of the key components and best practices related to device management and security in AWS IoT.

Device Registry and Device Shadows

AWS IoT Core maintains a **Device Registry**, which is a centralized repository for managing information about IoT devices. Each device is represented as a thing in the registry, and you can associate metadata, such as device type, serial number, and firmware version, with each thing. This registry allows you to keep track of all your devices, making it easier to manage and monitor them.

In addition to the device registry, AWS IoT Core supports **Device Shadows**, which are virtual representations of devices and their desired states. Device Shadows enable you to synchronize the state of a device in the cloud with the actual state of the device in the field. This is especially useful for managing devices that may go offline or have intermittent connectivity.

Device Authentication and Authorization

Device authentication and authorization are crucial for ensuring that only authorized devices can interact with your IoT solution. AWS IoT Core supports various authentication methods, including **X.509 certificates**, **SigV4 signatures**, and **custom authentication**. X.509 certificates are commonly used for device authentication and can be generated and managed using AWS IoT Core's certificate authority.

Once a device is authenticated, you can configure fine-grained access control using AWS IoT policies. **IoT policies** define what actions a device is allowed or denied to perform on specific AWS IoT resources. By creating and attaching policies to your devices, you can control who can access and perform operations on those devices.

Here's an example of an IoT policy that allows a device to publish data to a specific topic:

```
{
"Version": "2012-10-17",
"Statement": [
{
```

```
    "Effect": "Allow",
    "Action": "iot:Publish",
    "Resource":        "arn:aws:iot:us-east-1:1234567890:topic/my/
topic"
    }
  ]
}
```

Secure Device Communication

AWS IoT Core uses secure communication protocols to ensure the confidentiality and integrity of data exchanged between devices and the cloud. Devices can connect to AWS IoT Core using **MQTT** or **MQTT over WebSocket** for lightweight and efficient communication.

For secure communication, each device must present a valid certificate during the TLS handshake. AWS IoT Core verifies the certificate and ensures that the device is authorized to connect. Data sent between the device and AWS IoT Core is encrypted to protect it from eavesdropping.

Device Lifecycle Management

Managing the lifecycle of IoT devices is essential, especially when devices need to be provisioned, updated, or retired. AWS IoT Core provides tools for device provisioning, including the ability to use **just-in-time provisioning (JITP)** and automate the onboarding process.

Additionally, you can use **OTA (Over-the-Air) updates** to remotely update device firmware and software. This feature allows you to keep devices up to date with the latest security patches and features without physically accessing them.

Device Auditing and Monitoring

AWS IoT Core provides extensive auditing and monitoring capabilities to track device activities and detect anomalies. You can use **CloudWatch Logs** to capture logs generated by IoT devices and monitor metrics related to device connections and message publishing.

AWS IoT Device Defender is another service that helps you audit and monitor your device fleet for security-related issues. It can detect abnormal device behavior and alert you to potential security threats.

In summary, AWS IoT Core offers a comprehensive set of features and best practices for device management and security. By maintaining a device registry, implementing strong authentication and authorization, securing device communication, and effectively managing the device lifecycle, you can build secure and scalable IoT solutions on AWS.

Section 15.5: Building IoT Applications

In this section, we will delve into the process of building IoT applications using AWS services. IoT applications involve collecting data from various sensors and devices, processing that data, and taking actions based on it. AWS provides a rich set of services to simplify the development of IoT applications.

Data Ingestion and Storage

The first step in building an IoT application is ingesting data from devices. AWS IoT Core is designed for this purpose. It can receive data from a wide range of devices and protocols, making it easy to connect devices to the cloud.

Once data is ingested, you need a place to store it. **Amazon S3** is a highly scalable and durable object storage service that is commonly used for storing IoT data. You can organize data in S3 buckets and enable versioning and lifecycle policies to manage data retention.

Data Processing and Analytics

IoT data often requires processing and analysis to derive insights or trigger actions. **AWS Lambda** is a serverless compute service that can be used to process IoT data in real-time. For example, you can create Lambda functions that execute when new data arrives from a device, allowing you to perform custom processing or invoke other AWS services.

For more complex data processing and analytics tasks, **Amazon Kinesis** offers a set of services for real-time data streaming and analytics. **Amazon Kinesis Data Streams** can ingest and process large volumes of data, while **Amazon Kinesis Data Analytics** can be used to analyze and derive insights from the data stream.

Rules Engine and Actions

AWS IoT Core provides a **Rules Engine** that allows you to define rules for processing and routing IoT data. For instance, you can create rules that trigger actions when specific conditions are met. These actions can include invoking Lambda functions, storing data in databases, or sending notifications.

For more advanced routing and transformation of data, **AWS IoT Events** can be used. IoT Events enables you to detect events and trigger actions based on complex patterns in your data. It's particularly useful for detecting anomalies or identifying specific situations in your IoT data.

Device Control and Management

Managing and controlling IoT devices is crucial. With **AWS IoT Device Management**, you can track and manage your devices throughout their lifecycle. It provides features for onboarding, configuring, and monitoring devices at scale. You can also use Device Management to send remote commands to devices.

Visualization and Dashboards

To visualize IoT data and gain insights, **Amazon QuickSight** and **Amazon Quicksight** offer tools for creating dashboards and visualizations. You can use these services to build interactive dashboards that display real-time IoT data, helping you make informed decisions.

Security and Compliance

Security is paramount in IoT applications. AWS provides features like **AWS Identity and Access Management (IAM)** for fine-grained access control, and **Amazon Cognito** for authentication and user management. You should also implement security best practices like encrypting data in transit and at rest.

Regarding compliance, AWS services often comply with various industry standards and certifications, making it easier to build IoT applications that meet regulatory requirements.

Scalability and Availability

IoT applications often require high scalability and availability to handle fluctuating workloads. AWS services like **Amazon EC2 Auto Scaling** and **Amazon Aurora** can help you achieve scalability, while **AWS Global Accelerator** and **Amazon Route 53** provide options for distributing workloads and ensuring high availability across regions.

In conclusion, building IoT applications on AWS involves a combination of data ingestion, processing, rules-based actions, device management, visualization, and a strong focus on security and compliance. AWS offers a comprehensive set of services to simplify each aspect of IoT application development, enabling you to create robust and scalable solutions.

Chapter 16: Machine Learning on AWS

Section 16.1: AWS Machine Learning Services

Machine learning (ML) has become an integral part of modern applications, and AWS provides a suite of services to help you build, train, and deploy machine learning models at scale. In this section, we'll explore AWS machine learning services and understand how they can be leveraged for various use cases.

Amazon SageMaker

Amazon SageMaker is a fully managed service that simplifies the process of building, training, and deploying machine learning models. It provides a Jupyter Notebook interface for data scientists and developers to create ML models using popular frameworks like TensorFlow and PyTorch.

Key features of Amazon SageMaker include:

- **Managed Notebooks:** SageMaker offers pre-configured Jupyter notebooks with ML libraries and GPU support, making it easy to start experimenting with your data.

- **Built-in Algorithms:** It provides a wide range of built-in algorithms for common ML tasks like regression, classification, and clustering.

- **Model Training:** SageMaker can efficiently train models on large datasets, and you can easily scale training jobs to take advantage of distributed computing.

- **Hyperparameter Optimization:** It includes automated hyperparameter tuning to optimize your model's performance.

- **Model Deployment:** Once your model is trained, SageMaker simplifies deployment with built-in hosting services, allowing you to create RESTful endpoints for real-time predictions.

- **Monitoring and Management:** You can monitor deployed models for drift and performance using SageMaker Model Monitor.

Amazon Personalize

Amazon Personalize is a service for building personalized recommendations for your applications. It uses ML algorithms to create real-time recommendations, enabling you to deliver tailored content or product recommendations to your users.

Key features of Amazon Personalize include:

- **Real-time Recommendations:** Personalize provides APIs to retrieve real-time recommendations, making it suitable for applications like e-commerce, media streaming, and content delivery.

- **Customization:** You can customize recommendation models using your data to better suit your specific business needs.

- **Data Integration:** Personalize supports integration with Amazon S3, Amazon Redshift, and other data sources to gather the data needed for training recommendation models.

AWS Deep Learning AMIs

For deep learning enthusiasts, **AWS Deep Learning Amazon Machine Images (AMIs)** provide pre-configured environments with deep learning frameworks such as TensorFlow, PyTorch, MXNet, and more. These AMIs are optimized for GPU-based deep learning tasks.

Key features of AWS Deep Learning AMIs include:

- **Framework Support:** The AMIs come with popular deep learning frameworks pre-installed, reducing the setup time for deep learning projects.

- **GPU Acceleration:** They leverage GPU instances for accelerated model training.

- **Community and Enterprise Versions:** You can choose between community and enterprise versions, depending on your requirements.

Amazon Comprehend

Amazon Comprehend is a natural language processing (NLP) service that can analyze text data for sentiment analysis, entity recognition, and language detection. It's useful for applications involving text data, such as customer feedback analysis and content categorization.

Key features of Amazon Comprehend include:

- **Sentiment Analysis:** Comprehend can determine the sentiment (positive, negative, neutral) of text data.

- **Entity Recognition:** It can identify entities like names, dates, and locations in text.

- **Language Detection:** The service can automatically detect the language of the text.

- **Customization:** You can customize Comprehend for domain-specific use cases using custom entity recognition.

These are just a few examples of the machine learning services available on AWS. By leveraging these services, you can integrate machine learning capabilities into your applications without the need for extensive ML expertise, accelerating your ability to deliver intelligent, data-driven features to your users. In the subsequent sections of this chapter, we'll explore these services in more detail and provide examples of how to use them effectively.

Section 16.2: Amazon SageMaker

In the previous section, we introduced Amazon SageMaker as a comprehensive service for building, training, and deploying machine learning models on AWS. In this section, we will delve deeper into the key components and capabilities of Amazon SageMaker.

SageMaker Components

Amazon SageMaker consists of several core components that work together to streamline the machine learning workflow:

1. **Notebooks**: SageMaker provides Jupyter Notebook instances that come pre-configured with popular machine learning libraries like TensorFlow, PyTorch, and scikit-learn. Data scientists and developers can use these notebooks for data exploration, model development, and experimentation.

2. **Built-in Algorithms**: SageMaker offers a collection of

built-in machine learning algorithms, including linear regression, XGBoost, k-means clustering, and more. These algorithms can be used for a wide range of tasks without the need to write custom code.

3. **Training Jobs**: To train machine learning models, you can create SageMaker training jobs. These jobs can scale to handle large datasets and complex models, making it suitable for both single-machine training and distributed training across multiple instances.

4. **Hyperparameter Tuning**: SageMaker includes automatic hyperparameter tuning, which helps optimize your model's performance by searching for the best set of hyperparameters within defined ranges.

5. **Model Hosting**: After training your model, you can easily deploy it as an endpoint for real-time predictions. SageMaker handles the underlying infrastructure, auto-scaling, and monitoring, ensuring high availability and reliability.

6. **Model Monitor**: SageMaker Model Monitor enables you to detect data drift and model quality issues in deployed models. It continuously monitors the data used for predictions and alerts you if discrepancies are detected.

7. **Ground Truth**: For labeling tasks in supervised learning, SageMaker Ground Truth provides a platform for labeling datasets using human labelers or machine learning. This helps create high-quality training datasets.

SageMaker Workflow

Let's walk through a typical machine learning workflow using Amazon SageMaker:

1. **Data Preparation**: Begin by preparing your dataset.

SageMaker allows you to easily ingest data from various sources, including Amazon S3 buckets, Amazon RDS databases, and more.

2. **Notebook Development**: Use SageMaker's Jupyter Notebook instances to explore and preprocess your data. You can create and test machine learning models in the notebook environment.

3. **Model Training**: Once you've developed your model, create a SageMaker training job. You can choose from built-in algorithms or bring your own custom code. SageMaker automatically provisions the necessary compute resources and performs the training.

4. **Hyperparameter Tuning**: If desired, utilize SageMaker's hyperparameter tuning feature to optimize your model's hyperparameters. This automated process saves time and resources.

5. **Model Deployment**: After successful training, deploy your model as a SageMaker endpoint. This endpoint can be accessed via API calls, allowing you to integrate the model into your applications.

6. **Model Monitoring**: Activate SageMaker Model Monitor to continuously check the quality of predictions and detect data drift. If issues arise, you'll receive alerts.

7. **Scaling and Management**: SageMaker handles the scaling and management of deployed models, ensuring they remain available and performant. You can easily update models with new versions.

8. **Cleanup**: When you're done with your resources, SageMaker allows you to clean up instances, endpoints, and other resources to avoid unnecessary costs.

Example Code

Here's a simplified example of how to create a SageMaker training job using Python and the SageMaker SDK:

```python
import sagemaker
from sagemaker import get_execution_role
from sagemaker.estimator import Estimator
# Get the SageMaker execution role
role = get_execution_role()
# Specify the training data location in Amazon S3
training_data = 's3://your-s3-bucket/path/to/training/data'
# Create a SageMaker Estimator with a built-in algorithm (e.g., XGBoost)
estimator = Estimator(
role=role,
instance_count=1,
instance_type='ml.m4.xlarge',
image_name='174872318107.dkr.ecr.us-east-1.amazonaws.com/xgboost:latest',
output_path='s3://your-s3-bucket/path/to/output',
sagemaker_session=sagemaker.Session()
)
# Start the training job
estimator.fit({'train': training_data})
```

This code creates a SageMaker Estimator, specifies the training data location, and starts a training job using the XGBoost algorithm.

Amazon SageMaker provides a powerful and flexible environment for machine learning development and deployment. Whether you're working on classification, regression, recommendation systems, or other ML tasks, SageMaker can help streamline the process and accelerate your machine learning projects. In the following sections, we'll explore more advanced SageMaker features and use cases.

Section 16.3: Deep Learning on AWS

In this section, we'll explore the capabilities of Amazon SageMaker for deep learning, a subfield of machine learning that focuses on neural networks with multiple layers (deep neural networks). Deep learning has gained significant popularity due to its ability to solve complex problems such as image recognition, natural language processing, and more.

Deep Learning Frameworks

Amazon SageMaker supports popular deep learning frameworks, including TensorFlow, PyTorch, and Apache MXNet. These frameworks provide the tools and libraries necessary to design, train, and deploy deep neural networks. Users can choose the framework that best suits their project's requirements and their familiarity with a specific framework.

SageMaker for Deep Learning

SageMaker Built-in Algorithms

SageMaker offers built-in deep learning algorithms, making it easy to get started with common tasks like image classification and text sentiment analysis. For example, the built-in image classification algorithm can be used to train models for recognizing objects or patterns in images. You can customize and fine-tune these algorithms to suit your specific use case.

Custom Deep Learning Models

For more advanced use cases, you can build and train custom deep learning models using TensorFlow or PyTorch within SageMaker's

Jupyter Notebook environment. This flexibility allows data scientists and machine learning practitioners to experiment with various neural network architectures and hyperparameters.

Distributed Training

Deep learning models can be computationally intensive and require significant computational resources. SageMaker supports distributed training across multiple GPU instances, enabling faster model training. This distributed training can dramatically reduce the time required to train complex deep neural networks.

SageMaker Debugger

SageMaker Debugger is a tool that helps you monitor and debug deep learning models during training. It provides real-time insights into training metrics, gradients, and more, allowing you to identify and fix issues that may affect model performance.

Example Code

Here's an example of how to train a custom deep learning model for image classification using TensorFlow in Amazon SageMaker:

```python
import sagemaker
from sagemaker import get_execution_role
from sagemaker.tensorflow import TensorFlow
# Get the SageMaker execution role
role = get_execution_role()
# Specify the training script and dependencies
entry_point = 'train.py'
source_dir = 'source'
# Create a SageMaker TensorFlow Estimator
estimator = TensorFlow(
```

```
entry_point=entry_point,
source_dir=source_dir,
role=role,
framework_version='2.6.0',
py_version='py37',
instance_count=1,
instance_type='ml.p3.2xlarge',
hyperparameters={
'epochs': 10,
'batch-size': 64,
'learning-rate': 0.001
}
)
# Start the training job
estimator.fit({'training': 's3://your-s3-bucket/path/to/training/data'})
```

In this code, we create a SageMaker TensorFlow Estimator, specify the training script (train.py) and its dependencies, configure the training instance, and start the training job. The training data is stored in an Amazon S3 bucket.

Deep learning on Amazon SageMaker offers a scalable and flexible environment for building and training neural networks. Whether you're working on computer vision tasks, natural language processing, or any other deep learning application, SageMaker simplifies the process of training and deploying deep learning models. In the next section, we'll explore model deployment and monitoring in SageMaker.

Section 16.4: Model Deployment and Monitoring

Once you have trained a deep learning model using Amazon SageMaker, the next step is deploying it for real-world use. In this section, we'll explore the deployment options available and discuss how to monitor the deployed models for performance and accuracy.

Deployment Options

Amazon SageMaker provides several deployment options to suit different use cases:

Real-Time Inference

For real-time applications where low-latency predictions are required, you can deploy your deep learning model as an endpoint. SageMaker manages the underlying infrastructure, scaling it as needed to handle incoming inference requests. This allows you to integrate your model with web applications, mobile apps, or other services via API calls.

Batch Transform

If you have a large batch of data that needs inference, you can use SageMaker's batch transform feature. This is useful for scenarios such as batch processing of images or documents. You provide the input data, and SageMaker generates predictions for the entire dataset in a cost-effective manner.

Edge Deployment

In cases where you need to run deep learning models on edge devices such as IoT devices or edge servers, SageMaker Edge Manager helps you package and deploy models to these devices. It also provides capabilities for monitoring and managing models at the edge.

Model Monitoring

Monitoring the deployed model's performance is crucial to ensure it continues to provide accurate predictions. Amazon SageMaker provides the following tools for model monitoring:

Amazon CloudWatch

Amazon CloudWatch can be used to set up custom monitoring and alarms for your SageMaker endpoints. You can monitor key metrics such as inference latency, error rates, and request counts. If performance metrics deviate from predefined thresholds, you can receive alerts and take corrective actions.

SageMaker Model Monitor

SageMaker Model Monitor is a feature that automatically detects data quality issues and model drift. It helps you identify when the input data distribution or model behavior deviates significantly from what was observed during training. You can schedule regular monitoring jobs to ensure that your deployed model remains accurate over time.

Monitoring with Custom Scripts

For more customized monitoring requirements, you can implement custom monitoring scripts. These scripts can periodically evaluate the model's performance and trigger actions based on predefined conditions. Custom scripts offer flexibility in monitoring specific aspects of your application.

Continuous Integration and Continuous Deployment (CI/CD)

To ensure smooth updates and deployments of your deep learning models, you can set up CI/CD pipelines. Tools like AWS CodePipeline and AWS CodeDeploy can be integrated into your workflow to automate model deployment, testing, and monitoring. This ensures that your models are always up-to-date and performing as expected.

Example Code

Here's a simplified example of deploying a SageMaker model as an endpoint:

```python
# Deploy the trained model as an endpoint
predictor = estimator.deploy(
initial_instance_count=1,
instance_type='ml.m4.xlarge',
endpoint_name='my-deep-learning-endpoint'
)
# Use the predictor to make real-time predictions
result = predictor.predict(input_data)
# Delete the endpoint when no longer needed
predictor.delete_endpoint()
```

In this code, we deploy a trained model as an endpoint, make predictions, and then delete the endpoint when it's no longer in use.

Model deployment and monitoring are essential aspects of using deep learning models in production. Amazon SageMaker simplifies these processes and provides the necessary tools to ensure the reliability and accuracy of your deployed models. In the next section, we'll explore best practices and considerations for AI and ML on AWS.

Section 16.5: AI and ML Best Practices

In this final section of Chapter 16, we'll delve into best practices for AI (Artificial Intelligence) and ML (Machine Learning) on AWS. These practices are essential for ensuring the success, reliability, and maintainability of your AI and ML projects.

1. Data Quality and Preparation

Data is the lifeblood of any AI or ML project. Ensuring the quality, completeness, and consistency of your data is paramount. AWS offers services like AWS Glue for data preparation and transformation. Always begin with clean and well-structured data to avoid issues down the line.

2. Model Selection

Selecting the right algorithm or model architecture is crucial. AWS provides a wide range of pre-built models and services like Amazon SageMaker for building custom models. Understand your problem domain and choose an appropriate model type to avoid overfitting or underfitting.

3. Data Security and Compliance

Maintain data security and compliance with AWS services like AWS Identity and Access Management (IAM) and AWS Key

Management Service (KMS). Ensure that sensitive data is appropriately protected, and you comply with industry regulations.

4. Model Training

Leverage AWS's scalable infrastructure for model training. Use Amazon SageMaker for distributed training across multiple instances. Implement hyperparameter tuning to optimize model performance.

5. Testing and Validation

Implement rigorous testing and validation procedures. Use services like Amazon SageMaker Debugger to identify issues during training and Amazon SageMaker Model Monitor for drift detection. Evaluate model performance using metrics relevant to your use case.

6. Scalability and Deployment

Design your AI/ML solutions to scale with demand. Utilize AWS Auto Scaling for automatically adjusting resources based on traffic. Deploy models as endpoints or leverage serverless computing with AWS Lambda for cost-effective and scalable solutions.

7. Continuous Monitoring and Optimization

Continuously monitor your deployed models using Amazon CloudWatch and SageMaker Model Monitor. Set up alerts and automated actions to address issues promptly. Regularly retrain models with new data to keep them accurate.

8. Cost Optimization

Optimize costs by using AWS Cost Explorer to analyze spending. Leverage Reserved Instances and Savings Plans for predictable workloads. Implement cost allocation tags to track expenses by project or department.

9. Documentation and Collaboration

Document your AI/ML workflows, data pipelines, and model architectures. Encourage collaboration among data scientists, developers, and domain experts. AWS provides tools like AWS CodeCommit and AWS CodeBuild for version control and collaboration.

10. AI Ethics and Bias Mitigation

Be aware of ethical considerations and potential biases in your models. Implement fairness and bias detection tools, and regularly audit your AI systems to ensure they align with ethical standards.

11. Disaster Recovery and Backup

Implement disaster recovery plans for critical AI/ML workloads. Use AWS Backup for data protection and recovery. Ensure your systems can quickly recover from failures.

12. Training and Education

Invest in training and education for your team. AWS offers a wealth of training resources and certifications to enhance your AI and ML expertise.

13. Stay Informed

AI and ML are rapidly evolving fields. Stay informed about the latest developments, tools, and best practices. Participate in AWS re:Invent and other industry events to network and learn from experts.

By following these best practices, you'll be well-equipped to build, deploy, and maintain AI and ML solutions on AWS that deliver real value and maintain high standards of quality and compliance. In the final chapter of this book, we'll explore future trends and advanced topics in the world of AWS and cloud computing.

Chapter 17: AWS Migration and Hybrid Cloud

In this chapter, we will explore AWS migration strategies and hybrid cloud deployments. Migrating to the cloud can be a complex process, but AWS provides a variety of tools and services to help organizations seamlessly transition their workloads. Additionally, hybrid cloud architectures allow businesses to combine on-premises infrastructure with cloud resources, offering flexibility and scalability.

Section 17.1: Cloud Migration Strategies

Migrating to the cloud is a significant step for many organizations, and it requires careful planning and execution. AWS offers several migration strategies to choose from, depending on your specific needs and constraints.

1. Rehosting (Lift and Shift)

Rehosting involves moving your existing on-premises applications to AWS infrastructure with minimal changes. This strategy is suitable for organizations looking to quickly migrate and reduce infrastructure costs. Tools like AWS Server Migration Service (SMS) simplify this process by automating the replication and migration of virtual machines.

2. Replatforming (Lift, Tinker, and Shift)

Replatforming involves making slight adjustments to your applications to take advantage of cloud-native features. This strategy often includes optimizing the application for cloud scalability, reliability, and cost-effectiveness. Organizations may choose to move databases to Amazon RDS or utilize AWS managed services like Amazon Elastic Beanstalk for application deployment.

3. Refactoring (Rearchitecting)

Refactoring is a more extensive transformation of your applications to leverage cloud-native capabilities fully. This strategy involves rearchitecting your applications to use AWS services like AWS Lambda, Amazon S3, and Amazon DynamoDB. While it requires more effort, it can result in improved performance, scalability, and cost savings.

4. Rebuilding

Rebuilding is a strategy where you create entirely new cloud-native applications, often using AWS services and microservices architecture. While this approach provides the greatest flexibility and optimization, it also requires the most development effort. Organizations adopting a cloud-native mindset may choose this strategy for new projects.

5. Hybrid Cloud Deployments

In some cases, organizations may opt for a hybrid cloud approach, where they maintain some workloads on-premises and migrate others to the cloud. AWS offers services like AWS Outposts and AWS Snow Family to enable hybrid deployments, ensuring seamless integration between on-premises and cloud environments.

6. Data Migration

Regardless of the migration strategy, data migration is a critical component. AWS offers services such as AWS Database Migration Service (DMS) and AWS DataSync to facilitate the secure and efficient transfer of data to the cloud.

7. Testing and Validation

Throughout the migration process, rigorous testing and validation are essential. Organizations should conduct testing to ensure that applications function as expected in the cloud environment and meet performance and security requirements.

8. Cost Management

Cost management is another crucial aspect of migration. AWS Cost Explorer and AWS Trusted Advisor can help organizations optimize costs and ensure that they are taking full advantage of cost-saving opportunities in the cloud.

9. Security and Compliance

Maintaining security and compliance during migration is paramount. Organizations must configure AWS Identity and Access Management (IAM) policies, security groups, and network access control lists (NACLs) to secure their cloud resources. Additionally, AWS provides tools like AWS Config and AWS CloudTrail for monitoring and auditing.

10. Training and Skills Development

Investing in training and skill development for your IT and development teams is essential to ensure that they are proficient in AWS services and best practices for cloud migration and management.

In the subsequent sections of this chapter, we will delve deeper into specific AWS migration services and hybrid cloud deployment scenarios to provide you with a comprehensive understanding of how to navigate the complexities of cloud migration and hybrid cloud architecture.

Section 17.2: AWS Database Migration Service (DMS)

AWS Database Migration Service (DMS) is a powerful tool designed to simplify and streamline the process of migrating databases to AWS. It supports homogeneous migrations, where the source and target databases are of the same type, as well as heterogeneous migrations, allowing you to migrate between different database engines.

Key Features of AWS DMS

1. **Supported Source and Target Databases**: AWS DMS supports a wide range of source and target database engines, including MySQL, PostgreSQL, Oracle, SQL Server, MongoDB, and more. This flexibility allows you to migrate between different database types with ease.

2. **Continuous Data Replication**: DMS enables continuous data replication from the source database to the target database. Once replication is set up, changes made to the source database are automatically reflected in the target, ensuring minimal downtime during migration.

3. **Schema Conversion**: In heterogeneous migrations, where source and target databases have different schemas, AWS DMS can perform schema conversion. It maps data types, converts constraints, and ensures data consistency during the migration process.

4. **Table and Row-level Mapping**: You have fine-grained control over which tables and rows to migrate. AWS DMS allows you to filter data based on specific criteria, ensuring that only the required data is migrated.

5. **High Availability and Data Validation**: DMS provides high availability by supporting replication instance failover.

Additionally, it offers data validation features to verify that the data in the target database matches the source, ensuring data integrity.

6. **Change Data Capture (CDC)**: AWS DMS uses CDC to capture and replicate changes in real-time. This includes inserts, updates, and deletes, allowing for near real-time data synchronization.

7. **Zero-downtime Migration**: With AWS DMS, you can perform a migration with minimal downtime. During the migration, changes made to the source database are continuously replicated to the target. Once you're ready to switch, you can minimize the cutover time.

Steps to Perform a Database Migration with AWS DMS

Here are the general steps involved in performing a database migration using AWS Database Migration Service:

1. Create a Replication Instance

- Start by creating a replication instance, which acts as the conduit for data replication between the source and target databases. You can specify instance size, availability zone, and other configuration settings.

2. Configure Source and Target Endpoints

- Define the source and target endpoints. This involves providing connection details for the source and target databases, such as endpoint addresses, port numbers, and credentials.

3. Create a Migration Task

- Create a migration task that specifies what data to migrate and how to transform it if needed. You can select the tables to migrate, apply filtering, and define table and column mappings.

4. Start Data Replication

- Begin data replication by starting the migration task. AWS DMS will begin copying data from the source to the target database. You can monitor the progress and view replication statistics in the AWS Management Console.

5. Data Validation and Testing

- It's crucial to validate data integrity and functionality in the target database. AWS DMS provides features for comparing data between the source and target to ensure consistency.

6. Cutover to the Target Database

- Once you're satisfied with the data migration and validation, plan the cutover to the target database. This typically involves redirecting application traffic to the target database and finalizing the migration.

7. Post-migration Optimization

- After the migration is complete, you can optimize the target database for performance, security, and cost management. This may involve adjusting resource configurations and fine-tuning queries.

Benefits of Using AWS DMS

- **Minimized Downtime**: AWS DMS supports continuous data replication, reducing downtime during migrations and ensuring business continuity.

- **Database Independence**: You can migrate between different database engines, making it easier to adopt new technologies and take advantage of AWS-managed databases.

- **Data Consistency**: AWS DMS ensures that data remains consistent between the source and target databases, reducing the risk of data discrepancies.

- **Easy Monitoring**: The AWS Management Console provides real-time monitoring and replication status, allowing you to track the progress of your migration.

- **Cost-Effective**: AWS DMS is a cost-effective solution for database migrations, eliminating the need for expensive, time-consuming manual processes.

In summary, AWS Database Migration Service simplifies the process of migrating databases to AWS, offering flexibility, data integrity, and minimal downtime. Whether you're performing a homogeneous or heterogeneous migration, AWS DMS provides the tools and features needed for a successful transition.

Section 17.3: AWS Server Migration Service (SMS)

AWS Server Migration Service (SMS) is a specialized AWS service designed to simplify and automate the process of migrating on-premises servers, including virtual machines (VMs), to AWS. SMS streamlines server migrations by providing an agentless approach, enabling you to migrate servers with minimal disruption and downtime.

Key Features of AWS SMS

1. **Agentless Migration**: One of the significant advantages of AWS SMS is that it doesn't require you to install agents on your source servers. This means you can migrate your servers without making any changes to your existing infrastructure.

2. **Incremental Replication**: AWS SMS uses incremental replication to continuously replicate changes made to the source servers. This ensures that your target servers remain up to date, and you can cut over to AWS with minimal data loss.

3. **Integrated with AWS**: SMS is tightly integrated with other AWS services, making it easy to configure target Amazon Machine Images (AMIs) and launch new instances in Amazon EC2. You can leverage AWS resources for improved scalability, security, and cost management.

4. **Application Discovery**: AWS SMS includes an application discovery feature that helps you identify servers and their dependencies. This information is crucial for planning and executing a successful migration.

5. **Automation and Orchestration**: You can use SMS to

create and manage replication jobs, making it easier to automate the migration process. You can also orchestrate server migrations, ensuring that servers are migrated in the desired order.

6. **Migration Readiness Checks**: AWS SMS performs readiness checks to ensure that servers are suitable for migration. It identifies potential issues that could impact migration and provides recommendations for resolution.

Steps to Perform Server Migration with AWS SMS

Here's an overview of the steps involved in performing a server migration using AWS Server Migration Service:

1. Discover Servers: Begin by using AWS SMS to discover your on-premises servers and gather information about their configuration and dependencies.

2. Create Replication Jobs: Define replication jobs in AWS SMS to specify which servers to migrate and configure the replication settings. You can choose the replication frequency and target AWS region.

3. Configure Target AMIs: In AWS, configure target Amazon Machine Images (AMIs) that will be used to launch new EC2 instances. You can customize these AMIs to meet your application's requirements.

4. Test Migrations: Perform test migrations to ensure that the migration process works as expected and that the target EC2 instances are functioning correctly. This is a critical step to identify and resolve any issues.

5. Perform the Migration: Once you are confident in the migration process, initiate the migration jobs. AWS SMS will replicate data from your source servers to the target AWS region.

6. Cut Over to AWS: After the data replication is complete and you have verified the functionality of your target EC2 instances, you can schedule the cutover. During the cutover, you will redirect traffic to the AWS-hosted servers.

7. Post-Migration Optimization: Following the migration, optimize your AWS resources for performance, security, and cost management. You may need to adjust configurations and fine-tune your applications.

Benefits of Using AWS SMS

- **Minimized Downtime**: AWS SMS enables live migrations with minimal disruption to your business operations. You can keep your source servers running during the migration process.

- **Agentless Approach**: The agentless migration approach eliminates the need to install software on source servers, simplifying migration planning and execution.

- **Automated Replication**: SMS automates data replication, ensuring that your target EC2 instances stay synchronized with your on-premises servers.

- **Integration with AWS**: AWS SMS is tightly integrated with AWS services, allowing you to leverage cloud resources and take advantage of AWS features for security and scalability.

- **Application Discovery**: The application discovery feature helps you gain visibility into your server environment and understand dependencies, making it easier to plan migrations.

- **Migration Validation**: SMS performs readiness checks and allows you to conduct test migrations, helping you identify and address potential issues before migrating production workloads.

In summary, AWS Server Migration Service (SMS) simplifies the migration of on-premises servers to AWS by offering an agentless, automated, and integrated approach. This service streamlines the migration process and helps you ensure a successful transition to the cloud.

Section 17.4: Hybrid Cloud Deployments

Hybrid cloud deployments combine on-premises infrastructure with cloud resources, creating a flexible and scalable environment that allows organizations to leverage the benefits of both worlds. AWS offers a range of services and tools to support hybrid cloud architectures, enabling businesses to seamlessly extend their on-premises data centers to the cloud.

Key Components of a Hybrid Cloud

1. On-Premises Data Centers: The existing on-premises infrastructure serves as the foundation of a hybrid cloud deployment. This can include physical servers, storage, and networking equipment.

2. AWS Cloud: AWS provides the cloud component of the hybrid architecture. Organizations can use AWS services such as Amazon EC2, Amazon S3, and Amazon RDS to expand their computing and storage capabilities.

3. Connectivity: Establishing secure and reliable connectivity between on-premises data centers and the AWS cloud is crucial. AWS offers various options, including AWS Direct Connect, VPN connections, and Transit Gateway, to facilitate network integration.

4. Identity and Access Management: AWS Identity and Access Management (IAM) allows organizations to manage access to AWS resources securely. IAM policies can be configured to grant permissions to on-premises users and applications.

5. Data Integration: Organizations often need to transfer data between on-premises and cloud environments. AWS provides services like AWS DataSync and AWS Storage Gateway to simplify data migration and synchronization.

6. Application Deployment: Hybrid cloud architectures enable organizations to deploy applications across on-premises and cloud environments. AWS Elastic Beanstalk and AWS Lambda are examples of services that support hybrid application deployment.

Benefits of Hybrid Cloud Deployments

1. Scalability: Organizations can scale their computing resources up or down in response to changing demands. This flexibility is particularly valuable for applications with variable workloads.

2. Cost Optimization: Hybrid clouds allow organizations to optimize costs by leveraging the cost-effective and pay-as-you-go pricing model of the cloud while retaining control over existing on-premises infrastructure.

3. Business Continuity: By extending workloads to the cloud, organizations can enhance their disaster recovery and business continuity strategies. In the event of a data center failure, critical applications can failover to the cloud.

4. Global Reach: AWS offers a global network of data centers, allowing organizations to deploy resources in multiple geographic regions for low-latency access to global customers.

5. Innovation: The cloud provides access to a wide range of AWS services, including artificial intelligence, machine learning, and analytics. Organizations can innovate faster by leveraging these services in hybrid architectures.

6. Security and Compliance: AWS provides a secure and compliant cloud environment. Organizations can extend their security policies and controls to the cloud, ensuring data protection and regulatory compliance.

Use Cases for Hybrid Cloud Deployments

Hybrid cloud architectures are well-suited to various use cases, including:

1. Backup and Recovery: Organizations can use the cloud as a backup target for on-premises data, enabling fast and reliable data recovery.

2. Disaster Recovery: In the event of a disaster, critical applications and data can be replicated to the cloud for failover and continuity.

3. Data Processing: For data-intensive workloads, organizations can offload data processing tasks to the cloud to reduce on-premises resource requirements.

4. Testing and Development: Developers can provision cloud resources for testing and development, accelerating application development lifecycles.

5. Global Expansion: Companies looking to expand their operations globally can deploy applications in the cloud's global regions to serve local customers.

6. Seasonal Workloads: Retailers and e-commerce businesses can handle seasonal peaks in demand by scaling their infrastructure with cloud resources.

To implement a successful hybrid cloud deployment, organizations should carefully plan their architecture, assess their connectivity needs, and choose the right combination of on-premises and cloud resources. AWS provides a comprehensive set of tools and services to facilitate the integration of on-premises and cloud environments, making it easier for businesses to achieve the benefits of hybrid cloud computing.

Section 17.5: Cloud Adoption Framework

The **Cloud Adoption Framework (CAF)** is a set of guidelines and best practices provided by AWS to help organizations plan, design, and implement their cloud adoption journey successfully. It offers a structured approach to cloud adoption, enabling businesses to achieve their goals, whether it's improving agility, reducing costs, or enhancing innovation. In this section, we will explore the key components and principles of the Cloud Adoption Framework.

Core Components of the Cloud Adoption Framework

1. Perspectives: CAF encourages organizations to view cloud adoption from multiple perspectives, including business, people, governance, platform, security, and operations. Each perspective helps stakeholders understand the impact of cloud adoption on their respective areas.

2. Stakeholder Roles: Identifying and defining the roles of stakeholders within the organization is essential. CAF provides guidance on roles such as Cloud Business Office (CBO), Cloud Center of Excellence (CCoE), and Cloud Program Management Office (CPMO).

3. Guiding Principles: CAF defines a set of guiding principles that organizations should follow during their cloud adoption journey. These principles include aligning with business goals, securing from the start, and focusing on business value.

4. Business Case: Creating a strong business case for cloud adoption is crucial. It helps organizations justify the investment in cloud technology and provides a clear understanding of the expected benefits.

5. Readiness Assessments: CAF recommends conducting readiness assessments to evaluate the organization's preparedness for cloud adoption. These assessments cover areas such as governance, skills, and technology.

6. Landing Zones: Landing zones are the foundational environment where workloads are initially deployed in the cloud.

CAF provides landing zone blueprints and design principles to establish secure and well-architected environments.

7. Migration Strategies: CAF offers guidance on choosing the right migration strategy, whether it's rehost, refactor, rearchitect, rebuild, or replace. The goal is to optimize the migration process for minimal disruption.

8. Governance: Establishing robust governance practices is essential for managing cloud resources effectively. CAF provides governance frameworks and policies to ensure compliance, security, and cost management.

Key Principles of the Cloud Adoption Framework

1. Start from Business Goals: Cloud adoption should align with the organization's business objectives and strategic goals. It's not just an IT initiative; it's a strategic move that impacts the entire organization.

2. Think Big, Start Small: Organizations should start their cloud journey with manageable pilot projects before scaling up to more extensive deployments. This minimizes risks and allows for learning and adjustment.

3. Security is Job Zero: Security should be a top priority from the beginning of the cloud adoption process. CAF emphasizes the importance of building security into every aspect of cloud operations.

4. Enablement and Education: Cloud adoption requires upskilling the workforce. Organizations should invest in training and education programs to ensure that teams have the necessary skills and knowledge.

5. Automate Everything: Automation is a key enabler for agility and scalability. CAF encourages organizations to automate routine tasks and processes wherever possible.

6. Measure Everything: Effective cloud adoption requires continuous monitoring and measurement of key performance indicators (KPIs) to ensure that objectives are met and resources are optimized.

Benefits of Using the Cloud Adoption Framework

The Cloud Adoption Framework offers several benefits to organizations:

1. Structured Approach: CAF provides a structured and well-defined approach to cloud adoption, reducing the complexity and risks associated with migration.

2. Alignment with Best Practices: By following CAF guidelines, organizations align their cloud adoption strategy with industry best practices and AWS recommendations.

3. Risk Mitigation: CAF helps organizations identify and mitigate potential risks early in the cloud adoption process, ensuring a smoother transition.

4. Cost Optimization: The framework promotes cost-effective cloud usage through governance and cost management practices.

5. Agility and Innovation: CAF enables organizations to become more agile and innovative by leveraging the scalability and capabilities of the cloud.

In conclusion, the Cloud Adoption Framework is a valuable resource for organizations embarking on their cloud journey with AWS. It provides a roadmap, best practices, and a set of principles to guide organizations through the process of adopting cloud technologies effectively. By following CAF's structured approach, businesses can maximize the benefits of the cloud while minimizing risks and disruptions.

Chapter 18: AWS Well-Architected Framework

Section 18.1: Principles of Well-Architected Design

The **AWS Well-Architected Framework** is a set of best practices and guidelines for building secure, high-performing, resilient, and efficient infrastructure for your applications. It's designed to help you make informed decisions and understand the potential impact of those decisions on your systems. This section focuses on the key principles of well-architected design that form the foundation of the framework.

1. Security

Security is the first and foremost principle of well-architected design. It's essential to protect your data and systems from unauthorized access and ensure data privacy and compliance. Key aspects of security in well-architected design include:

- **Data Protection**: Implement encryption, access controls, and secure key management to protect data at rest and in transit.

- **Identity and Access Management (IAM)**: Use IAM to manage user and application access to AWS resources, following the principle of least privilege.

- **Network Security**: Leverage VPCs, security groups, and network ACLs to isolate and control network traffic effectively.

2. Reliability

Reliability ensures that your systems can recover from failures and continue to function as expected. Well-architected design principles for reliability include:

- **Multi-Availability Zone (AZ) Deployments**: Distribute your workload across multiple AZs to enhance fault tolerance.

- **Monitoring and Recovery**: Implement robust monitoring, alerting, and automated recovery mechanisms to quickly detect and respond to issues.

- **Backup and Restore**: Regularly back up critical data and have a well-defined plan for data recovery.

3. Performance Efficiency

Optimizing performance is crucial to deliver a responsive user experience and cost-effective solutions. Key considerations for performance efficiency include:

- **Resource Optimization**: Choose the right instance types, storage options, and database engines to match your workload's requirements.

- **Scalability**: Design your architecture to scale horizontally or vertically to handle changes in load.

- **Caching**: Implement caching strategies to reduce latency and improve response times.

4. Cost Optimization

Cost optimization involves managing and optimizing your AWS resources to ensure you get the best value for your investment. Principles for cost optimization include:

- **Right Sizing**: Select the right resource sizes to match your workload's needs, avoiding overprovisioning.

- **Usage Monitoring**: Continuously monitor resource usage and implement cost allocation tags for tracking expenses.

- **Reserved Instances (RIs) and Savings Plans**: Utilize RIs and Savings Plans to reduce costs for predictable workloads.

5. Operational Excellence

Operational excellence focuses on optimizing operations and processes. Key components of operational excellence in well-architected design are:

- **Documentation**: Maintain detailed documentation for your systems, including runbooks and standard operating procedures.

- **Automation**: Implement automation for routine tasks and infrastructure management to reduce manual effort.

- **Resource Lifecycle Management**: Efficiently manage the lifecycle of resources, including provisioning, scaling, and decommissioning.

Benefits of Well-Architected Design

By adhering to the principles of well-architected design, organizations can realize several benefits:

- **Enhanced Security**: Protect sensitive data and applications from threats and vulnerabilities.

- **Improved Reliability**: Ensure systems can recover quickly from failures and continue to operate without disruptions.

- **Optimized Performance**: Deliver a faster and more responsive user experience.

- **Cost Savings**: Reduce unnecessary spending on resources and infrastructure.

- **Operational Efficiency**: Streamline operations and reduce manual tasks through automation.

In conclusion, the AWS Well-Architected Framework provides a structured approach to designing and managing cloud architecture that meets the highest standards of security, reliability, performance, cost efficiency, and operational excellence. By incorporating these principles into your cloud solutions, you can build robust and efficient systems that drive business success.

Section 18.2: AWS Well-Architected Tool

The **AWS Well-Architected Tool** is a service provided by AWS to help you review and improve your workloads following the best practices of the AWS Well-Architected Framework. It guides you through a set of questions and provides recommendations based on your responses, helping you align your architecture with the framework's principles. In this section, we'll explore the AWS Well-Architected Tool and how you can leverage it to assess and optimize your cloud workloads.

Using the AWS Well-Architected Tool

1. Accessing the Tool

To access the AWS Well-Architected Tool, you can log in to your AWS Management Console and navigate to the AWS Well-Architected Tool dashboard. Alternatively, you can use the AWS Command Line Interface (CLI) or AWS SDKs to interact with the tool programmatically.

2. Workload Selection

Once you're in the tool, you can select the specific workload or application you want to assess. You can also choose to create a new workload if you're starting from scratch.

3. Reviewing Pillars

The AWS Well-Architected Tool is organized around the five pillars: Security, Reliability, Performance Efficiency, Cost Optimization, and Operational Excellence. For each pillar, the tool will present a set of questions and best practice guidelines.

4. Assessment and Recommendations

As you answer the questions for each pillar, the tool assesses your workload against best practices. It provides recommendations, identifies areas for improvement, and highlights potential risks.

These recommendations are based on AWS's experience with thousands of customers and workloads.

5. Actionable Insights

The tool not only identifies issues but also provides actionable insights and resources to help you address them. It might suggest AWS services, documentation, or reference architectures that can assist you in implementing best practices.

6. Prioritization and Planning

The recommendations come with guidance on prioritization, helping you focus on the most critical improvements first. You can also create an action plan and track your progress in the tool.

Benefits of the AWS Well-Architected Tool

1. Alignment with Best Practices: The tool ensures your workloads align with the AWS Well-Architected Framework, which can enhance the security, reliability, and efficiency of your applications.

2. Risk Identification: It helps you identify potential risks and issues in your architecture, enabling proactive risk mitigation.

3. Resource Optimization: By following the tool's recommendations, you can optimize your resource usage and reduce unnecessary costs.

4. Operational Efficiency: The tool promotes operational excellence by suggesting automation and process improvements.

5. Continuous Improvement: With the tool's regular assessments, you can continuously improve your workloads over time, adapting to changing requirements and technologies.

Integrating with AWS Solutions

The AWS Well-Architected Tool can be integrated into your AWS environment seamlessly. You can use it in conjunction with other AWS services and solutions, such as AWS Trusted Advisor and AWS Config, to gain a comprehensive view of your infrastructure and ensure it remains well-architected.

In summary, the AWS Well-Architected Tool is a valuable resource for organizations looking to optimize their cloud workloads. It provides a structured approach to assess, improve, and maintain the architecture of your applications, helping you achieve the highest standards of security, reliability, performance, cost efficiency, and operational excellence in the AWS cloud.

Section 18.3: Reviewing and Optimizing Architectures

In this section, we'll delve into the process of reviewing and optimizing AWS architectures. Ensuring that your cloud architecture is well-architected is essential for achieving the desired performance, reliability, security, and cost efficiency of your workloads. The AWS Well-Architected Framework provides a set of best practices and principles for creating and maintaining a well-architected architecture. Let's explore the key steps involved in reviewing and optimizing your AWS architectures.

1. Architecture Review Process

Reviewing and optimizing your AWS architecture should be an iterative process. It involves the following key steps:

a. Identification: Begin by identifying the specific AWS architectures or workloads that need review. You may prioritize based on criticality, cost, or performance impact.

b. Documentation: Document the current state of your architecture. Create architectural diagrams, inventory lists, and descriptions of your resources and configurations. This documentation will serve as a baseline for your review.

c. Assessment: Use the AWS Well-Architected Framework as a guide. Assess your architecture against the five pillars: Security, Reliability, Performance Efficiency, Cost Optimization, and Operational Excellence. AWS provides a set of questions and best practices for each pillar.

d. Gap Analysis: Identify gaps or areas where your architecture does not align with best practices. These gaps may involve security vulnerabilities, performance bottlenecks, cost inefficiencies, or operational challenges.

e. Prioritization: Prioritize the identified gaps based on their impact on your business goals and the severity of the issues. Some issues may need immediate attention, while others can be addressed over time.

f. Optimization: Develop an optimization plan that includes specific actions to address the identified gaps. This plan may involve configuring resources, implementing security measures, optimizing code, or adjusting configurations.

g. Implementation: Execute the optimization plan systematically. Ensure that changes are well-documented and follow best practices. Monitor the impact of changes on your architecture.

2. Tools and Services

AWS provides various tools and services that can assist in the architecture review and optimization process:

- AWS Well-Architected Tool: This tool offers a structured way to assess and optimize architectures, aligning them with the Well-Architected Framework.

- AWS Trusted Advisor: It provides real-time guidance to help you optimize your resources for cost, performance, security, and fault tolerance.

- AWS Config: AWS Config helps you assess the compliance of your architecture with desired configurations and track changes over time.

- AWS CloudWatch: Monitor the performance of your resources and applications, allowing you to identify performance bottlenecks that need optimization.

- AWS Cost Explorer: Analyze your AWS spending to identify areas where cost optimization is possible.

3. Continuous Improvement

Optimizing your AWS architecture is not a one-time task but an ongoing process. Cloud architectures evolve, and new best practices emerge. It's crucial to maintain a culture of continuous improvement, regularly reviewing and optimizing your architectures to adapt to changing requirements and technologies.

4. Best Practices

To optimize your AWS architecture effectively, follow these best practices:

- Regularly review your architecture against the AWS Well-Architected Framework.

• Implement automation for resource provisioning and scaling to achieve operational excellence.

• Use AWS identity and access management (IAM) to enforce security best practices.

• Leverage AWS-native services for cost optimization and performance improvements.

• Monitor your architecture's performance using AWS CloudWatch and other monitoring tools.

• Implement redundancy and failover mechanisms to enhance reliability.

• Keep documentation up to date to support architectural reviews.

In conclusion, reviewing and optimizing AWS architectures is a critical aspect of maintaining a well-architected cloud environment. By following a structured review process, leveraging AWS tools and services, and adopting best practices, you can ensure that your architectures align with business goals, stay secure, and remain cost-effective and performant.

Section

Section 18.5: Cost Optimization Strategies

While security and performance are essential considerations in AWS, cost optimization is equally crucial. In this section, we'll explore various strategies to help you optimize your AWS spending without sacrificing performance or security.

1. Use AWS Cost Explorer

AWS provides a tool called Cost Explorer that helps you visualize and analyze your AWS spending. It offers various reports, cost breakdowns, and forecasting capabilities. By regularly monitoring your spending patterns using Cost Explorer, you can identify cost-saving opportunities.

2. Leverage Cost Allocation Tags

Tags are metadata that you can assign to your AWS resources. Utilize cost allocation tags to categorize resources by department, project, or purpose. This makes it easier to track costs and allocate expenses accurately, enabling better cost control and optimization.

3. Rightsize Your Resources

One common source of overspending is provisioning resources with more capacity than needed. Use AWS tools like Amazon CloudWatch and AWS Trusted Advisor to identify underutilized resources. You can then resize or terminate instances accordingly to match your actual workload requirements.

4. Reserved Instances (RIs) and Savings Plans

RIs and Savings Plans offer significant cost savings compared to on-demand pricing. Analyze your usage patterns and commit to RIs or Savings Plans for resources that have consistent workloads. AWS offers various types of RIs and flexible Savings Plans to suit different needs.

5. Spot Instances and Spot Fleets

For non-critical workloads that can tolerate interruptions, consider using Spot Instances and Spot Fleets. These resources are available at significantly lower prices than on-demand instances but may be reclaimed with short notice.

6. Use Auto Scaling Effectively

Auto Scaling helps you automatically adjust the number of instances based on workload changes. Set up Auto Scaling groups to ensure you have the right number of instances running at any given time, reducing costs during periods of low demand.

7. Data Transfer Costs

Be mindful of data transfer costs, especially when transferring data outside AWS regions or over the public internet. Use AWS Direct Connect or Virtual Private Network (VPN) connections to reduce data transfer costs for large data transfers.

8. Storage Optimization

Regularly review your storage requirements. Consider using Amazon S3's storage classes to automatically move data to more cost-effective storage tiers as it ages. Also, delete unneeded snapshots, backups, or objects to free up storage and reduce costs.

9. Elastic Load Balancing

Choose the appropriate type of Elastic Load Balancer (ELB) based on your needs. Application Load Balancers (ALB) and Network Load Balancers (NLB) offer different features and pricing. Select the one that aligns with your use case to optimize costs.

10. Implement a Cost Optimization Culture

Encourage your team to adopt a cost-conscious mindset. Conduct regular cost reviews, set budgets, and promote awareness of the cost implications of different AWS services and resource choices.

11. Consider Serverless and Managed Services

Serverless computing and managed services like AWS Lambda, Amazon RDS, and AWS Fargate often provide cost benefits because you pay only for actual usage. Evaluate if these services can replace or complement existing infrastructure.

12. Continuous Monitoring and Optimization

Cost optimization is an ongoing process. Continuously monitor your AWS usage, analyze cost reports, and implement adjustments as needed. AWS Trusted Advisor and third-party cost optimization tools can assist in this process.

By implementing these cost optimization strategies, you can ensure that your AWS spending remains under control while still meeting your performance and security requirements. Remember that optimizing costs doesn't mean compromising on the quality of your AWS resources; it's about efficiently allocating resources to match your actual needs.

Chapter 19: Case Studies and Real-World Scenarios

In this chapter, we'll delve into various real-world case studies and scenarios where organizations have successfully leveraged Amazon Web Services (AWS) to solve unique challenges and achieve their goals. These stories serve as valuable examples of how AWS can be applied across different industries and use cases.

Section 19.1: Case Study: Building a High-Performance Website

Introduction

In this case study, we'll explore how a startup company achieved exceptional website performance and scalability using AWS services. The company, which offers an innovative online platform, faced the challenge of handling rapid growth in user traffic while maintaining low latency and high availability.

Challenges

The startup's challenges included:

1. **High Traffic**: The website experienced rapid growth in user traffic, leading to performance issues during peak hours.
2. **Low Latency**: Users demanded low-latency access to content and services, necessitating a globally distributed infrastructure.
3. **Scalability**: The platform needed to scale horizontally to accommodate increasing loads and maintain responsiveness.

AWS Solutions

To address these challenges, the startup adopted the following AWS solutions:

1. **Amazon CloudFront**: AWS's content delivery network (CDN) service helped reduce latency by caching and serving content from edge locations worldwide.
2. **Amazon Elastic Load Balancing (ELB)**: ELB evenly distributed incoming traffic across multiple Amazon EC2 instances, ensuring high availability and scalability.
3. **Amazon RDS**: The company used Amazon RDS for managed relational databases, simplifying database management and ensuring data consistency.
4. **Amazon Route 53**: Route 53 provided scalable and highly available DNS services, ensuring reliable domain name resolution.
5. **Amazon EC2 Auto Scaling**: Auto Scaling automatically adjusted the number of EC2 instances based on traffic, ensuring optimal performance during traffic spikes.

Results

By implementing these AWS services, the startup achieved the following outcomes:

- **Improved Website Performance**: Latency significantly decreased, resulting in a better user experience.

- **High Availability**: The website became more resilient to traffic fluctuations and server failures.

- **Scalability**: The company could easily accommodate increasing numbers of users without compromising performance.

- **Cost Efficiency**: AWS's pay-as-you-go pricing model allowed the startup to manage costs efficiently.

This case study illustrates how AWS services can be harnessed to overcome challenges related to website performance and scalability, making it a valuable resource for organizations aiming to provide high-quality online experiences to their users.

Section 19.2: Real-World Data Analytics with AWS

In this section, we'll explore a real-world scenario where a data-driven company leveraged AWS to implement a powerful data analytics platform. The organization faced the challenge of processing and analyzing vast amounts of data from various sources to gain valuable insights and make data-driven decisions.

Challenges

The company encountered several challenges in their data analytics journey:

1. **Data Variety**: Data was sourced from diverse channels, including databases, logs, social media, and IoT devices, leading to data silos.
2. **Scalability**: Traditional on-premises solutions struggled to handle the increasing volume of data.
3. **Cost**: Managing infrastructure and storage costs for on-premises data centers became unsustainable.

AWS Solutions

To address these challenges, the company implemented a comprehensive AWS-based data analytics solution:

1. **Amazon S3**: They used Amazon S3 as a central data lake to store all types of data in its raw format, making it accessible for analysis.
2. **Amazon EMR (Elastic MapReduce)**: EMR allowed them to process and analyze large datasets using Apache Spark and Hadoop, enabling distributed data processing.
3. **Amazon Redshift**: For complex data warehousing and querying needs, Amazon Redshift provided a scalable and high-performance solution.
4. **AWS Glue**: AWS Glue automated the ETL (Extract, Transform, Load) process, making data ingestion and transformation more efficient.
5. **Amazon QuickSight**: QuickSight served as the business intelligence tool for data visualization and reporting.

Results

By leveraging these AWS services, the organization achieved significant outcomes:

• **Unified Data**: Amazon S3 acted as a central repository, breaking down data silos and providing a unified view of data.

• **Scalability**: AWS's scalability allowed them to process and analyze increasing amounts of data without upfront investments.

- **Cost Optimization**: The pay-as-you-go model and serverless capabilities reduced infrastructure and management costs.

- **Data Insights**: With faster data processing and analytics, the company gained valuable insights, enabling data-driven decision-making.

This real-world scenario highlights how AWS services can empower organizations to build efficient, scalable, and cost-effective data analytics platforms, ensuring they can extract valuable insights from their data resources.

Section 19.3: IoT Implementation Success Story

In this section, we'll delve into an IoT (Internet of Things) implementation success story where a company effectively leveraged AWS IoT services to transform their operations. IoT offers powerful capabilities to collect, process, and act upon data from connected devices, creating new opportunities and efficiencies.

Challenges

The organization faced several challenges that are common in the IoT landscape:

1. **Device Management**: Managing a large number of IoT devices efficiently and securely.
2. **Data Volume**: Handling the massive volume of data generated by devices in real-time.
3. **Scalability**: Ensuring the infrastructure can scale to accommodate a growing number of devices and data.
4. **Security**: Implementing robust security measures to

protect both devices and data.

AWS IoT Solutions

To address these challenges, the company adopted AWS IoT services, including:

1. **AWS IoT Core**: The core IoT service that provides device management, security, and data ingestion capabilities.
2. **AWS IoT Analytics**: To process and analyze IoT data in real-time and derive insights.
3. **AWS Lambda**: For serverless computing to trigger actions based on IoT data.
4. **Amazon S3**: To store and archive IoT data securely.
5. **Amazon QuickSight**: For creating interactive dashboards and visualizing IoT data.

Results

By implementing AWS IoT services, the company achieved remarkable results:

- **Efficient Device Management**: AWS IoT Core simplified device onboarding, authentication, and management.

- **Real-time Insights**: The ability to process data in real-time allowed for immediate actions and insights.

- **Scalability**: The architecture easily scaled to accommodate more devices and data volume.

- **Enhanced Security**: AWS IoT's built-in security features provided robust protection for both devices and data.

- **Cost Optimization**: The pay-as-you-go model reduced infrastructure costs.

This success story illustrates how AWS IoT services enable organizations to overcome the challenges associated with IoT deployments and unlock the potential of connected devices, ultimately leading to improved operational efficiency and innovative solutions.

In conclusion, the combination of AWS IoT Core, IoT Analytics, serverless computing with AWS Lambda, and other AWS services can empower organizations to harness the full potential of IoT, drive operational improvements, and create new opportunities in various industries.

Section 19.4: Machine Learning in Healthcare

In this section, we explore the applications of machine learning (ML) in healthcare, highlighting how AWS provides tools and services to facilitate the adoption of ML in this critical domain.

The Promise of Machine Learning in Healthcare

Machine learning has the potential to revolutionize healthcare by enabling more accurate diagnoses, personalized treatments, and efficient healthcare operations. It can analyze vast amounts of medical data, including electronic health records (EHRs), medical images, and genomic data, to uncover insights that can improve patient outcomes and streamline healthcare processes.

AWS Machine Learning Services

AWS offers a suite of machine learning services and tools that are well-suited for healthcare applications:

1. **Amazon SageMaker**: This fully managed service makes it easy to build, train, and deploy ML models. Healthcare practitioners and researchers can use SageMaker to develop predictive models for diseases, drug discovery, and treatment optimization.
2. **Amazon Comprehend Medical**: This service is designed specifically for healthcare and can extract medical information from unstructured text, such as clinical notes and medical literature. It helps automate the process of organizing and analyzing medical text data.
3. **Amazon Rekognition**: For medical imaging, Amazon Rekognition can analyze medical images, such as X-rays and MRIs, to detect anomalies and assist radiologists in their diagnoses.
4. **AWS Deep Learning AMIs**: These Amazon Machine Images (AMIs) come pre-installed with deep learning frameworks, making it easier for healthcare researchers to train and deploy deep learning models on AWS.

Use Cases

Machine learning in healthcare has numerous use cases, including:

- **Disease Prediction**: ML models can analyze patient data to predict disease risk, allowing for early intervention and preventive care.

- **Medical Imaging**: ML can enhance medical image analysis by automating the identification of abnormalities and aiding radiologists in their assessments.

- **Drug Discovery**: ML accelerates drug discovery by analyzing molecular data and predicting the efficacy of potential drugs.

- **Personalized Treatment**: ML models can recommend personalized treatment plans based on a patient's medical history and genetic information.

- **Operational Efficiency**: ML helps healthcare organizations optimize resource allocation, patient scheduling, and supply chain management.

Ethical Considerations

While ML offers immense benefits in healthcare, it also raises ethical and privacy concerns, particularly regarding patient data security and bias in algorithms. AWS provides tools and guidelines to ensure the responsible and ethical use of AI and ML in healthcare.

Conclusion

The integration of machine learning into healthcare on the AWS platform holds great promise for improving patient care, diagnosis accuracy, and operational efficiency. As healthcare organizations continue to adopt these technologies, it is crucial to strike a balance between innovation and ethical considerations to realize the full potential of ML in healthcare.

Section 19.5: Lessons from Real AWS Projects

In this section, we delve into real-world case studies and projects that have leveraged Amazon Web Services (AWS) to solve complex challenges across various domains. These projects offer valuable insights and lessons for organizations looking to harness the power of AWS for their initiatives.

Case Study 1: High-Performance Website

Challenge: A media company needed to scale their website to handle traffic spikes during major events. They also wanted to improve website performance and reduce latency for global users.

Solution: AWS Elastic Load Balancing (ELB) and Amazon CloudFront were used to distribute traffic efficiently and cache content at edge locations. Amazon RDS ensured database scalability. Auto Scaling groups were employed to dynamically adjust resources based on traffic.

Lessons Learned: Autoscaling and content caching are essential for handling variable traffic loads and improving user experience. Implementing a content delivery network (CDN) reduces latency and enhances global accessibility.

Case Study 2: Real-Time Data Analytics

Challenge: An e-commerce company required real-time insights into user behavior to optimize product recommendations and inventory management.

Solution: AWS Lambda, Amazon Kinesis, and Amazon Redshift were used to process and analyze streaming data. AWS Glue facilitated data preparation, while Amazon QuickSight provided visualization of analytics.

Lessons Learned: Serverless and real-time data processing can deliver actionable insights. Leveraging managed services simplifies data pipeline management.

Case Study 3: IoT Implementation

Challenge: A manufacturing firm aimed to enhance equipment monitoring and predictive maintenance using IoT.

Solution: AWS IoT Core was employed to connect and manage IoT devices. AWS Lambda processed device data, and Amazon S3 stored historical data. Machine learning models for predictive maintenance were built with Amazon SageMaker.

Lessons Learned: AWS IoT Core simplifies IoT device management. Combining IoT with machine learning can prevent equipment failures.

Case Study 4: Healthcare Data Analytics

Challenge: A healthcare provider wanted to improve patient care by analyzing electronic health records (EHRs) for patterns and anomalies.

Solution: AWS data analytics services like Amazon EMR and Amazon Athena were used to process EHR data. Machine learning models were created to predict disease risks.

Lessons Learned: Cloud-based data analytics accelerates insights from EHRs, leading to better patient care. Security and compliance must be prioritized when dealing with sensitive healthcare data.

Case Study 5: Machine Learning in Finance

Challenge: A financial institution sought to enhance fraud detection and risk assessment using machine learning.

Solution: AWS services like Amazon SageMaker and AWS Lambda enabled the development and deployment of ML models for real-time fraud detection. AWS Step Functions orchestrated complex workflows.

Lessons Learned: ML can significantly improve security and risk management in finance. Orchestrating workflows with Step Functions streamlines processes.

Conclusion

These real-world AWS projects demonstrate the versatility and scalability of AWS services across diverse industries. Organizations can learn from these case studies to design and implement solutions that meet their unique needs while leveraging the power of the cloud and cutting-edge technologies. Successful AWS projects require a combination of well-chosen services, effective architecture, and adherence to best practices for security and scalability.

Chapter 20: Future Trends and Advanced Topics

Section 20.1: Emerging AWS Services and Technologies

In this section, we explore the cutting-edge AWS services and technologies that are shaping the future of cloud computing. AWS is constantly innovating to provide solutions that address evolving industry demands and enable businesses to stay competitive. Here, we highlight some of the emerging AWS offerings and trends that organizations should be aware of.

1. AWS Outposts

AWS Outposts is a game-changer for organizations that require low-latency access to AWS services within their own data centers. It extends the AWS infrastructure to on-premises locations, providing a consistent hybrid cloud experience. This enables businesses to run AWS services on their own hardware while seamlessly connecting to the broader AWS ecosystem.

2. AWS Quantum Computing

Quantum computing is on the horizon, and AWS is at the forefront of this emerging technology. **AWS Braket** is a fully managed quantum computing service that allows researchers and developers to experiment with quantum algorithms. While quantum computing is still in its infancy, its potential impact on industries like cryptography and materials science is significant.

3. AWS Wavelength

For applications that require ultra-low latency, **AWS Wavelength** delivers AWS services to the edge of the 5G network. This allows developers to build applications that can benefit from the high-speed, low-latency capabilities of 5G. Use cases include augmented and virtual reality, IoT, and real-time gaming.

4. AWS App Runner

AWS App Runner is a fully managed container service that simplifies the process of building, deploying, and scaling containerized applications. It abstracts away much of the underlying infrastructure management, making it easier for developers to focus on their code. This service is ideal for microservices architectures.

5. AWS Distro for OpenTelemetry

Observability is crucial for modern applications. **AWS Distro for OpenTelemetry** helps developers instrument their applications for tracing and monitoring. It's designed to work seamlessly with AWS services, providing deep insights into application performance and reliability.

6. AWS Copilot

Developers can streamline containerized application deployment with **AWS Copilot**, a command-line tool that automates many of the repetitive tasks involved in building, testing, and releasing containerized applications. It's an excellent tool for accelerating the development of containerized applications on AWS.

7. AI and Machine Learning Advancements

AWS continues to invest heavily in AI and machine learning. **Amazon SageMaker Studio** provides a fully integrated development environment for building, training, and deploying ML models. The **AWS Inferentia** chip accelerates deep learning inference workloads, making AI applications faster and more cost-effective.

8. Serverless Trends

Serverless computing is evolving with more advanced offerings. **AWS Proton** simplifies the deployment and management of serverless applications, while **AWS Step Functions** is increasingly used for orchestrating complex serverless workflows.

9. AWS Sustainability Initiatives

As sustainability becomes a global priority, AWS is committed to reducing its carbon footprint. The **AWS Sustainability Hub** helps organizations measure, report, and reduce their environmental impact while running workloads in the cloud.

Conclusion

AWS's commitment to innovation ensures that businesses have access to the latest technologies and services. Staying informed about emerging AWS offerings is essential for organizations looking to leverage the cloud to drive innovation, optimize operations, and gain a competitive edge in a rapidly changing landscape. Embracing these trends and technologies can position businesses for success in the future of cloud computing.

Section 20.2: Quantum Computing and AWS

In this section, we delve into the fascinating world of quantum computing and how AWS is actively involved in advancing this cutting-edge technology. Quantum computing holds immense promise for solving complex problems that are practically impossible for classical computers to tackle. AWS has recognized the potential of quantum computing and has launched AWS Braket, a service that allows researchers, scientists, and developers to experiment with and harness the power of quantum computers.

Understanding Quantum Computing

Quantum computing leverages the principles of quantum mechanics to perform computations in ways that classical computers cannot. Classical computers use bits as the basic unit of information, representing either a 0 or a 1. Quantum computers, on the other hand, use quantum bits or qubits, which can exist in multiple states simultaneously due to a phenomenon called superposition. This property allows quantum computers to process vast amounts of data and perform complex calculations much faster than classical computers for certain types of problems.

AWS Braket: Quantum Computing as a Service

AWS Braket is a fully managed service that provides access to quantum computing resources. It allows users to explore and experiment with quantum algorithms, simulators, and quantum hardware from leading quantum computing providers such as Rigetti, IonQ, and D-Wave. AWS Braket simplifies the process of conducting quantum experiments by handling many of the complexities of quantum computing, such as error correction and calibration.

Example Code for AWS Braket

```python
from braket.circuits import Circuit
    from braket.devices import LocalSimulator
    # Create a quantum circuit
    circuit = Circuit().h(0).cnot(0, 1)
```

```
# Simulate the circuit on a local quantum simulator
simulator = LocalSimulator()
result = simulator.run(circuit, shots=1000).result()
# Get measurement results
counts = result.measurements
print(counts)
```

In this code example, we create a simple quantum circuit that applies a Hadamard gate (h) and a controlled-not gate (cnot) to two qubits. We then use the LocalSimulator provided by AWS Braket to simulate the circuit and obtain measurement results.

Quantum Computing Use Cases

Quantum computing has the potential to revolutionize various fields, including cryptography, materials science, drug discovery, and optimization problems. Some quantum computing use cases include:

- **Cryptography**: Quantum computers can break commonly used encryption methods, but they also offer the potential for quantum-safe encryption methods.

- **Materials Science**: Quantum simulations can help discover new materials with unique properties, leading to advancements in electronics, energy storage, and more.

- **Drug Discovery**: Quantum computing can significantly accelerate the discovery of new drugs by simulating molecular interactions and drug-binding properties.

- **Supply Chain Optimization**: Quantum algorithms can optimize complex supply chain and logistics problems, reducing costs and improving efficiency.

- **Financial Modeling**: Quantum computing can be used for risk assessment, portfolio optimization, and financial modeling, allowing for more accurate predictions.

Conclusion

Quantum computing is still in its early stages, and practical, large-scale quantum computers are not yet widely available. However, AWS Braket enables researchers and developers to explore this exciting technology, experiment with quantum algorithms, and prepare for a future where quantum computing becomes an integral part of solving complex problems in various domains. AWS's commitment to advancing quantum computing ensures that businesses and researchers have the tools they need to harness the power of quantum mechanics for the benefit of society.

Section 20.3: Advanced Networking and Security

In this section, we explore advanced networking and security features and services offered by AWS. As businesses increasingly rely on the cloud to run their operations, ensuring robust network connectivity and security becomes paramount.

Advanced Networking with AWS

Virtual Private Cloud (VPC)

AWS provides Virtual Private Cloud (VPC), which allows you to create isolated, logically segmented networks within the AWS cloud environment. VPCs offer advanced networking capabilities such as custom IP address ranges, subnets, route tables, and network access control lists (NACLs). You can also establish peering connections between VPCs or connect your on-premises network to AWS using VPN or Direct Connect.

Amazon Route 53

Amazon Route 53 is a highly scalable and available Domain Name System (DNS) web service. It not only helps you route traffic to your AWS resources but also to on-premises resources. You can use Route 53 for domain registration, DNS health checks, and global load balancing.

Advanced Security with AWS

AWS Identity and Access Management (IAM)

IAM allows you to control access to your AWS resources securely. With advanced IAM features, you can set fine-grained permissions, use identity federation for single sign-on (SSO), and implement multi-factor authentication (MFA) for enhanced security.

AWS WAF and AWS Shield

AWS Web Application Firewall (WAF) helps protect your web applications from common web exploits and attacks. AWS Shield provides DDoS (Distributed Denial of Service) protection, shielding your applications from network and transport layer attacks.

Amazon Inspector and AWS Trusted Advisor

Amazon Inspector automates security assessments of your AWS resources to identify vulnerabilities and security issues. AWS Trusted

Advisor offers real-time guidance to optimize your AWS environment for cost, performance, and security.

Networking and Security as Code

To manage advanced networking and security configurations efficiently, you can use Infrastructure as Code (IAC) tools like AWS CloudFormation and AWS CDK (Cloud Development Kit). These tools allow you to define your network and security configurations in code, enabling versioning, automation, and consistency.

Example AWS CDK Code for VPC

```
import * as cdk from 'aws-cdk-lib';
    import * as ec2 from 'aws-cdk-lib/aws-ec2';
    const app = new cdk.App();
    const stack = new cdk.Stack(app, 'AdvancedNetworkingStack');
    const vpc = new ec2.Vpc(stack, 'MyVpc', {
    maxAzs: 2, // Create VPC with 2 availability zones
    subnetConfiguration: [
    {
    cidrMask: 24,
    name: 'PublicSubnet',
    subnetType: ec2.SubnetType.PUBLIC,
    },
    {
    cidrMask: 24,
    name: 'PrivateSubnet',
    subnetType: ec2.SubnetType.PRIVATE,
    },
    ],
    });
    // Define security groups, route tables, and more as code
```

In this example, we use the AWS CDK to define a VPC with specified configurations, including public and private subnets.

Conclusion

Advanced networking and security are critical components of any AWS deployment. By leveraging AWS's advanced networking services, such as VPC and Route 53, and security services like IAM, WAF, and Shield, you can build secure and resilient applications in the cloud. Additionally, using Infrastructure as Code tools like AWS CloudFormation and AWS CDK simplifies the management of complex networking and security setups, making them reproducible and maintainable. These advanced networking and security features empower organizations to confidently operate in the cloud while meeting compliance and security requirements.

Section 20.4: Cloud Native and Serverless Trends

In this section, we'll delve into the evolving landscape of cloud-native and serverless computing, two prominent trends that are reshaping the way applications are developed, deployed, and managed in the cloud.

The Shift to Cloud-Native Architectures

Cloud-Native: Cloud-native refers to an approach where applications are designed and built to leverage the full potential of cloud computing. This approach emphasizes agility, scalability, and resilience. Key characteristics include microservices architecture, containerization, and continuous delivery.

Microservices Architecture

Microservices break down applications into smaller, loosely coupled services that can be developed and scaled independently. This approach enhances agility, allowing organizations to update and deploy components faster.

Containers and Orchestration

Containers, often managed using platforms like Docker and Kubernetes, package applications and their dependencies together. Container orchestration tools automate the deployment, scaling, and management of containerized applications, ensuring high availability.

DevOps and CI/CD

DevOps practices and CI/CD pipelines are central to cloud-native development. Continuous integration (CI) and continuous deployment (CD) processes enable automated testing, integration, and delivery of code changes.

The Rise of Serverless Computing

Serverless: Serverless computing abstracts server management, allowing developers to focus solely on code. It automatically scales and manages the underlying infrastructure, reducing operational overhead.

AWS Lambda

AWS Lambda is a leading serverless compute service. It enables you to run code in response to events, such as HTTP requests or changes to data in Amazon S3. You pay only for the compute time used, with no need to provision or manage servers.

Event-Driven Architecture

Serverless applications are often event-driven, reacting to events generated by various sources. This architecture is well-suited for scenarios like real-time data processing and IoT applications.

Pros and Cons

Cloud-Native Pros

- **Scalability**: Easily scale components independently.
- **Resilience**: Fault tolerance through redundancy.
- **Speed**: Faster development and deployment cycles.
- **Cost Efficiency**: Optimize resource usage.

Cloud-Native Cons

- **Complexity**: Managing microservices and containers can be complex.
- **Learning Curve**: Requires new development and operational skills.
- **Operational Overhead**: Automation is essential but adds complexity.

Serverless Pros

- **Simplicity**: Focus on code, not infrastructure.
- **Automatic Scaling**: No need to manage server capacity.
- **Cost Savings**: Pay only for actual usage.

- **Rapid Development**: Accelerate development cycles.

Serverless Cons

- **Cold Starts**: Slight latency when initializing functions.
- **Resource Limitations**: Limited control over underlying resources.
- **Vendor Lock-In**: Code can be tightly coupled to a specific provider.

Combining Cloud-Native and Serverless

Many organizations find value in combining cloud-native and serverless approaches. For example, you can build cloud-native microservices but use serverless functions for specific tasks within those services, achieving a balance between control and simplicity.

Conclusion

Cloud-native and serverless computing represent significant shifts in cloud technology. Embracing these trends can help organizations build more agile, cost-effective, and resilient applications. However, it's crucial to carefully evaluate the suitability of these approaches for specific use cases and consider the associated trade-offs. Ultimately, the choice between cloud-native and serverless should align with your organization's goals and application requirements.

Section 20.5: Preparing for the Future of Cloud Computing

As cloud computing continues to evolve rapidly, it's essential for organizations to stay informed about emerging trends and technologies. Preparing for the future of cloud computing involves understanding the direction in which the industry is heading and making strategic decisions to remain competitive and efficient. In this section, we'll explore some of the key considerations for preparing your organization for the future of cloud computing.

Embracing Emerging Technologies

Edge Computing

Edge computing is becoming increasingly important as organizations seek to reduce latency and process data closer to the source. This approach involves deploying compute resources at the edge of the network, such as IoT devices or remote locations. AWS offers services like AWS IoT Greengrass to facilitate edge computing.

Quantum Computing

While still in its infancy, quantum computing has the potential to revolutionize computing power. AWS is actively exploring quantum computing technologies and offers services like Amazon Braket to experiment with quantum algorithms. Keeping an eye on quantum computing developments can help your organization stay ahead.

Advanced Networking and Security

As workloads become more distributed, advanced networking and security solutions become crucial. AWS provides services like AWS Transit Gateway for simplified network management and AWS Network Firewall for enhanced security. Understanding and adopting these technologies can improve your infrastructure's resilience and security.

Evolving Skills and Training

To navigate the future of cloud computing, your team needs to acquire new skills and stay updated on industry trends. AWS offers a variety of training resources, including AWS Training and Certification, to help your team build expertise in cloud technologies. Consider creating a training plan to ensure your staff is well-prepared for the challenges ahead.

Monitoring and Optimization

Continuous monitoring and cost optimization are key to future-proofing your cloud infrastructure. Leverage AWS monitoring and management tools like Amazon CloudWatch and AWS Trusted Advisor to gain insights into your usage and optimize costs. Regularly review your architecture to identify areas for improvement.

Embracing Cloud-Native and Serverless

Cloud-native and serverless computing are likely to continue growing in importance. Consider how these approaches can benefit your organization's specific use cases. Evaluate the trade-offs and determine where they fit within your overall cloud strategy.

Conclusion

The future of cloud computing promises exciting opportunities but also comes with its share of challenges. By staying informed about emerging technologies, investing in training and skill development, optimizing your cloud resources, and embracing cloud-native and serverless approaches, you can position your organization for success in the ever-evolving landscape of cloud computing. Remember that AWS provides a wide range of services and resources to support your journey and keep you at the forefront of innovation in the cloud industry.